2 -

The Apparatus of Death

By the Editors of Time-Life Books

Alexandria, Virginia

TIME
LIFE ®

Time-Life Books is a division of
Time Life Inc., a wholly owned subsidiary of

The Time Inc. Book Company
Time-Life Books

Managing Editor: Thomas H. Flaherty
Director of Editorial Resources:
Elise D. Ritter-Clough
Director of Photography and Research:
John Conrad Weiser
Editorial Board: Dale M. Brown, Roberta Conlan,
Laura Foreman, Lee Hassig, Jim Hicks, Blaine
Marshall, Rita Thievon Mullin, Henry Woodhead

PUBLISHER: Joseph J. Ward

Associate Publisher: Ann M. Mirabito
Editorial Director: Russell B. Adams, Jr.
Marketing Director: Anne C. Everhart
Director of Design: Louis Klein
Production Manager: Prudence G. Harris
Supervisor of Quality Control: James King

Editorial Operations
Production: Celia Beattie
Library: Louise D. Forstall
Computer Composition: Deborah G. Tait
(Manager), Monika D. Thayer,
Janet Barnes Syring, Lillian Daniels

The Cover: Locked inside a cattle car destined for
a death camp, two women catch their last glimpse
of freedom through an air vent secured with
barbed wire. To realize Adolf Hitler's fantasy of a
racially pure Europe, the Nazis waged genocide
against Jews and other people deemed undesirable. The final toll of innocent victims reached as
high as 15 million.

This volume is one of a series that chronicles
the rise and eventual fall of Nazi Germany. Other
books in the series include:
The SS
Fists of Steel
Storming to Power
The New Order
The Reach for Empire
Lightning War
Wolf Packs
Conquest of the Balkans
Afrikakorps
The Center of the Web
Barbarossa
War on the High Seas
The Twisted Dream
The Road to Stalingrad
The Shadow War
The Heel of the Conqueror
The Southern Front

The Third Reich

SERIES EDITOR: Henry Woodhead
Series Administrator: Philip Brandt George
Editorial Staff for *The Apparatus of Death:*
Senior Art Director: Raymond Ripper
Picture Editor: Jane Jordan
Text Editors: Paul Mathless, John Newton
Writer: Stephanie A. Lewis
Associate Editors/Research: Katya Sharpe Cooke,
Oobie Gleysteen
Assistant Editors/Research: Maggie Debelius,
Katherine Griffin
Assistant Art Director: Lorraine D. Rivard
Senior Copy Coordinator: Ann Lee Bruen
Picture Coordinator: Jennifer Iker
Editorial Assistant: Alan Schager

Special Contributors: Ronald H. Bailey,
Charles S. Clark, Kenneth C. Danforth, Lydia
Preston Hicks, Marge duMond, Peter Pocock,
David S. Thomson (text); Martha Lee Beckington,
Kevin A. Mahoney, Danielle S. Pensley, Marilyn
Murphy Terrell (research); Roy Nanovic (index)

Correspondents: Elisabeth Kraemer-Singh
(Bonn), Christine Hinze (London), Christina
Lieberman (New York), Maria Vincenza Aloisi
(Paris), Ann Natanson (Rome). Valuable
assistance was also provided by: Angelika
Lemmer (Bonn), Marlin Levin (Jerusalem),
Elizabeth Brown, Katheryn White (New York),
Michal Donath (Prague), Traudl Lessing (Vienna),
Bogdan Turek, Jarek Zuk (Warsaw).

First printing. Printed in U.S.A.

Published simultaneously in Canada.
School and library distribution by Silver Burdett
Company, Morristown, New Jersey 07960.

TIME-LIFE is a trademark of Time Warner Inc.
U.S.A.

**Library of Congress Cataloging in
Publication Data**
The Apparatus of death / by the editors of
Time-Life Books.
    p.   cm. — (The Third Reich)
Includes bibliographical references and index.
ISBN 0-8094-7004-7
ISBN 0-8094-7005-5 (lib. bdg.)
    1. Holocaust, Jewish (1939-1945).
2. Jews—Germany—History—1939-1945.
3. Auschwitz (Poland: Concentration camp).
4. World War, 1939-1945—Gypsies.
I. Time-Life Books. II. Series.
D804.3.A67 1991   940.53'18'0943—dc20   90-19702

Other Publications:

THE NEW FACE OF WAR
HOW THINGS WORK
WINGS OF WAR
CREATIVE EVERYDAY COOKING
COLLECTOR'S LIBRARY OF THE UNKNOWN
CLASSICS OF WORLD WAR II
TIME-LIFE LIBRARY OF CURIOUS AND UNUSUAL FACTS
AMERICAN COUNTRY
VOYAGE THROUGH THE UNIVERSE
THE TIME-LIFE GARDENER'S GUIDE
MYSTERIES OF THE UNKNOWN
TIME FRAME
FIX IT YOURSELF
FITNESS, HEALTH & NUTRITION
SUCCESSFUL PARENTING
HEALTHY HOME COOKING
UNDERSTANDING COMPUTERS
LIBRARY OF NATIONS
THE ENCHANTED WORLD
THE KODAK LIBRARY OF CREATIVE PHOTOGRAPHY
GREAT MEALS IN MINUTES
THE CIVIL WAR
PLANET EARTH
COLLECTOR'S LIBRARY OF THE CIVIL WAR
THE EPIC OF FLIGHT
THE GOOD COOK
WORLD WAR II
HOME REPAIR AND IMPROVEMENT
THE OLD WEST

For information on and a full description of any
of the Time-Life Books series listed above, please
call 1-800-621-7026 or write:
Reader Information
Time-Life Customer Service
P.O. Box C-32068
Richmond, Virginia 23261-2068

General Consultants

Col. John R. Elting, USA (Ret.), former associate professor at West Point, has written
or edited some twenty books, including
*Swords around a Throne, The Superstrate-
gists,* and *American Army Life,* as well as
Battles for Scandinavia in the Time-Life
Books World War II series. He was chief con-
sultant to the Time-Life series The Civil War.

Jon M. Bridgman, Professor of Military History at the University of Washington, spe-
cializes in the WWII period. He is the author
of numerous works on the subject, including
The Revolt of the Hereros and *The End of the
Holocaust: The Liberation of the Camps.*

Sybil Milton, Resident Historian for the
United States Holocaust Memorial Council,
has edited, translated, and written numerous books and articles on the Holocaust, including *The Stroop Report, Art of the Holocaust,* and *The Camera as Weapon and
Voyeur: Photography of the Holocaust as Historical Evidence.*

Contents

Innocents
Before
the Storm

Gypsy children play a game of
jump rope behind their caravans
at Unna, in German Westphalia,
in 1930. Laws restricting Gypsy
movement and camping places
had been issued as early as 1919
in Germany. In 1941, the policy
changed to that of extermination.

In 1932, youngsters frolic in the courtyard of Cologne's Abraham Frank House, a Jewish orphanage. On July 20, 1942, the children of the Frank House were deported to Minsk, in German-occupied Russia, and murdered on arrival by the SS.

Their talmudic studies ended for the day, Orthodox youngsters stroll along a street in Mukachevo, an old center of Jewish learning, in 1938. In the spring of 1944, the 200,000 Jews of the region were deported to the killing camp of Auschwitz.

The Shape of the "Final Solution"

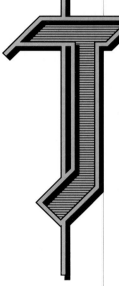

These were not the highest officials of the Third Reich but the leaders of the bureaucracy, the men who ran the daily affairs of Nazi Germany. On January 20, 1942, fifteen of them gathered for a luncheon meeting in a luxurious villa in the Berlin suburb of Wannsee. Among the party members present were the under secretary of the Foreign Office, secretaries in the Ministries of Justice and Interior, deputies from the departments that controlled newly conquered regions in the East, and key officials of the police agencies. These men were for the most part a cultured and highly educated group, a far cry from the street thugs who made up the old Sturmabteilung (SA), or Storm Troopers. The chairman of the meeting, Reinhard Heydrich, was an accomplished violinist; by dint of their extensive university studies, no fewer than seven of the participants could be addressed as "Herr Doktor."

Heydrich, the virtuoso deputy to Heinrich Himmler, chief of the elite Schutzstaffel, or SS, called the meeting to order at noon. He reminded his listeners that six months earlier he had been empowered by Reich Marshal Hermann Göring, who served as Adolf Hitler's deputy and acted on his direct orders, to organize a "complete solution of the Jewish question." The purpose of this Wannsee conference, he told the assembled group, was to coordinate the efforts of all the relevant ministries, departments, and agencies in implementing this task.

In a businesslike manner, using a chart as a visual aid, Heydrich presented a country-by-country breakdown of the 11 million Jews that he estimated lived in Europe. According to the minutes of the meeting, which were kept by his efficient expert in Jewish affairs, Adolf Eichmann, Heydrich announced that all these Jews would be taken to camps in the East "for labor utilization." As a result, he went on, "doubtless a large part will fall away through natural reduction." As for the survivors, "the toughest element," they "will have to be dealt with appropriately," he added.

After listening to Heydrich's brief blueprint for dealing with the Jews, the participants added their own ideas. Martin Luther, under secretary in the Foreign Office, proposed deportation plans for several areas of Europe.

Munich firemen lackadaisically inspect the charred and smoking remains of a synagogue, one of hundreds torched in Germany during an anti-Semitic rampage by Nazi Storm Troopers on the night of November 9, 1938. The Brownshirts smashed the windows of so many Jewish shops that the spasm of violence subsequently became known as the Night of Broken Glass.

Josef Bühler, deputy leader of the German-occupied region of Poland called the Government General, urged that the nearly two and a half million Jews now living there be given priority since "transport there played no major role." Otto Hofmann, chief of the SS Race and Settlement Office (RUSHA), joined a discussion of complicated legal questions—how to treat Jews married to non-Jews and how to deal with the *Mischlinge*, or Germans of so-called mixed race who had a single Jewish parent or grandparent.

Later, while butlers circulated among them with cocktails, the guests broke into small groups and discussed what the minutes of the conference describe as "various types of solution possibilities." Eichmann, who acted as the recording secretary, refrained from enumerating these possibilities. His minutes effectively obscure the language of the meeting with such bureaucratic euphemisms and circumlocutions as "natural selection" and the "final solution." In fact, as Eichmann admitted nineteen years later at his trial for war crimes, the luncheon guests spoke "in absolutely blunt terms—they addressed the issue, with no mincing of words." What the Wannsee conference was all about, he acknowledged, was "killing, elimination, and annihilation."

The killing had already begun. By the time of the conference, more than one million Jews, Slavs, and others had been shot, gassed, or killed through overwork, starvation, and disease. But most of these murderous efforts had been locally organized, especially on the eastern frontier. The Wannsee gathering signaled the inauguration of a systematic, comprehensive, and unprecedented program aimed at the extermination of an entire people.

After lunch and the departure of most of the guests, Heydrich relaxed. Having given impetus to the Nazi campaign of genocide with dispassionate talk of such details as rolling stock and railroad timetables, he sat in front of a fireplace in the villa drinking with two of his subordinates. Eichmann, who had jumped at the opportunity to socialize with both Heydrich and his own Gestapo chief, Heinrich Müller, recalled the scene vividly: "We sang songs. After awhile, we got up on the chairs and drank a toast, then on the table, and then round and round—on the chairs and on the table again. Heydrich taught it to us. It was an old north German custom." Then they sat quietly, Eichmann noted, "not just talking shop, but giving ourselves a rest after so many taxing hours."

The fury of the German government's final solution burned with such all-consuming fire that the killing of the Jews came to be known as the Holocaust. Between 5 and 6 million Jews perished in the Holocaust, close to 60 percent of Europe's prewar Jewish population. In its magnitude and systematic nature, the Holocaust was an event without parallel in human

In this 1819 engraving, Frankfurt residents attack two Jewish men while hussars ride past to quell the anti-Semitic brawl. The persecution of Jews in Germany scarcely began with Hitler; it was a phenomenon centuries old.

history. Jews were not the only victims in the appalling apparatus of death created by Nazi Germany. The identical mechanisms—neglect and mal-treatment as well as gas chambers and execution squads—claimed more than 10 million others who fell into Nazi hands during World War II. In fact, estimates of the toll of non-Jewish civilians killed by the Nazis run as high as 13 million. The number includes several hundred thousand Gypsies, Jehovah's Witnesses, Marxists, homosexuals, and others killed for religious, racial, or political reasons; most of all, it takes into account the often-forgotten 6 million Poles and millions of Slavs in the Soviet Union. In addition to these civilians, more than 3 million Slavs who were taken prisoner by the Germans while serving in the Soviet army are believed to have died in captivity.

Such mass extermination far from the combat zone resulted in large part from the deeply rooted racism that lay at the heart of Nazi ideology. Hitler's doctrine of German racial superiority allowed him to dictate the eradica-tion of those peoples he considered undesirable—above all, the Jews. It also gave him license to expand the Reich eastward and attain Lebensraum, or living space, for his master race at the expense of those who resided in his path of conquest.

The persecution of the Jews that attained such tragic dimensions in Nazi Germany had ancient beginnings. For many centuries, Christians through-out Europe had sought to convert the Jews to what they regarded as the one true religion. Failing in this, they created social and legal barriers, such as the prohibition of intermarriage, to discriminate against adherents to Judaism. During the Middle Ages in particular, Jews were segregated in ghettos, forcibly expelled, and murdered individually or en masse in massacres known as pogroms.

So intensely passionate was this religious intolerance that it gripped even such a towering figure as Martin Luther, the German theologian who broke with Catholicism in the sixteenth century and led the Protestant Reformation. In language venomous enough to please even Hitler four centuries later, Luther reviled the Jews as "a plague, a pestilence, a pure misfortune for our country," and labeled them "thirsty bloodhounds and murderers of all Christendom." His prescription for their treatment prefigured that adopted by later Germans: Burn their homes and synagogues and urge their deportation.

What Luther regarded as a religious issue eventually took on racial dimensions. By the nineteenth century, some European scholars were finding fault not just with the religious beliefs and practices of the Jews but with their biology as well. The Jews were a distinct race, it was said, and their behavior the result of immutable genetic characteristics. In the newly coalesced German Empire, writers seized on these racial theories to feed the rising fever of nationalism with a further conclusion: Jews formed an inferior race, Germans a superior one. For terminology to lend a scientific ring to their musings, the German racists looked to linguistics. The word *Aryan*, which they applied to themselves, originally denoted the Indo-European group of languages; the word *Semitic* referred to the language group that includes Hebrew and Arabic.

Among the most prominent of the writers who preached what now could be called anti-Semitism was an eccentric half-German, Houston Stewart Chamberlain. The son of a British admiral and a German mother, Chamberlain gained instant credibility in Germany by marrying the daughter of the revered composer Richard Wagner. Chamberlain's 1,200-page opus, *Foundations of the Nineteenth Century*, borrowed from the then-current craze for phrenology a means of differentiating race by measuring the length of the skull. Through such reasoning, he claimed he could distinguish a degenerate Jewish race and the master race of Aryans or Teutons, who represented all enlightenment. After its publication in 1899, Chamberlain's book became an immediate bestseller and drew praise from the kaiser himself, Wilhelm II, for bringing "order to confusion, light to darkness, and proof of what we suspected."

The racial aspects of anti-Semitism became further ensnared in the German nationalist mystique of the *Volk*. The word *Volk* means "people," but in the definition set forth late in the eighteenth century by the German philosopher Johann Gottfried von Herder, it took on a metaphysical meaning. Herder saw the German Volk as an eternal system of values, an unchanging spiritual ideal based on emotion rather than rationality and rooted in the agrarian way of life. A vague *völkisch* ideology, presaging the notion of blood and soil espoused by the Nazis, evolved as a conservative reaction to urbanization and democratic mass politics. The nostalgic ways of the past became linked with the idea of the Aryan race; the Jews came to stand for all that the völkisch ideologues abhorred— liberalism, urbanism, and modernism itself. Such cerebral outbreaks of racism did little to deter the enthusiasm of Jews for being German.

In November 1923, Germans turned in their worthless inflated marks for the new *Rentenmark.* The old note above was one of many saved and overprinted with the bitter complaint: "The Jews have the Rentenmark and gold! They are the winners again, and Christians are left with useless money." After World War I, Jews were blamed for everything from losing the war to inflation.

For the first time since their forebears had set foot on German soil in Roman times, the new constitution of 1871 had given them full legal equality. That event elicited from a Jewish member of the Prussian lower house the joyous declaration that "finally, after years of waiting in vain, we have landed in a safe harbor." And to thousands of Jews fleeing the pogroms of eastern Europe around the turn of the twentieth century, Germany seemed a haven indeed. German Jews, flourishing in business, science, and other professions now fully open to them for the first time, became the most assimilated of all European Jews. After Germany went to war in 1914, close to 15 percent of the nation's 540,000 Jews proudly rallied to the colors in defense of the kaiser and his empire. But in postwar defeat, the idea of Germany as a safe harbor for Jews echoed with cruel irony in the chaos of a crippled nation, and slowly began to crumble.

Hitler rose to prominence during the 1920s as the self-proclaimed destroyer of the Jewish dream of acceptance in Germany. Born in 1889, he had come of age in Vienna when the raging virus of racial hatred infected the radical political fringes of his native Austria as well as Germany. Anti-Semitic by conviction, the fledgling Führer pragmatically perceived the need for an all-purpose enemy to provide a focus for his political struggle. His reading of the history of revolutions, Hitler told a German journalist in 1922, had taught him to look around for a "lightning rod that could conduct and channel the odium of the general masses."

That age-old target, the Jew, became the lightning rod, and hatred of him the incandescent center of Hitler's National Socialist party philosophy. Hitler and the Nazis loudly blamed the Jews for every trouble that afflicted Germany during the 1920s: defeat in the war, the harsh terms imposed by the Treaty of Versailles, the problems of the Weimar government, the political appeal of Marxism, runaway inflation, economic depression, political corruption, and modern art. "Hatred, burning hatred," wrote Hitler in 1921. "This is what we want to pour into the souls of millions of fellow Germans, until the flame of rage ignites in Germany and avenges the corrupters of our nation."

A related aspect of German racial ideology—the drive for living space—also served as a foundation for nazism and the mass killing that was to take place later. The concept of Lebensraum was introduced in the late nineteenth century by Friedrich Ratzel, a German professor of political geography, who insisted that living space represented the state's most vital requirement. By 1927, when Hitler proclaimed Germany's need for Lebensraum in his book *Mein Kampf,* the idea had become enmeshed in racism. As the master race destined to live out their völkisch destiny on the soil, Hitler proclaimed, Germans deserved to expand their borders eastward all the way to the Ural Mountains of the Soviet Union. The people who stood in the way—200 million Slavs, along with a few million Jews—were racially inferior. "Slavs are a mass of born slaves," wrote Hitler, who referred to them as *Untermenschen,* or subhumans. To make way for the racially pure Aryan settlers, he decreed, one-third of the Slavs would be driven farther eastward into Asia, one-third would be reduced to slavery, and one-third would be liquidated.

Implementing the Lebensraum vision would have to await the war and conquest of the eastern lands, but Nazi persecution of the Jews began as soon as Hitler came to power in 1933. Slightly more than 500,000 Jews lived in Germany at the beginning of the Third Reich, making up less than one percent of the total population. The Führer would launch an officially sanctioned campaign of terror, economic pressure, and legislation intended to isolate them as enemies of the people. January 30, 1933, the fateful day on which Hitler was appointed chancellor, stamped an indelible impression on many Jews. One who would survive the Holocaust, Leslie Frankel, then a ten-year-old living in a village near Worms, remembered

On April 1, 1933, a Storm Trooper stands watch outside a Jewish store in Berlin during a nationwide one-day boycott of Jewish businesses. In an effort to silence foreigners who criticized Germany's treatment of Jews, the SA posted signs in English implying that Jewish claims of persecution were false.

that he had been ice-skating that afternoon. "When I got home," he recalled, "we heard that Hitler had become chancellor. Everybody shook. As kids of ten we shook."

The primary instruments of terror in the early days of Nazi power were the brown-shirted bullies of the Sturmabteilung. Since their formation in 1921, the Storm Troopers had engaged in random acts of violence against Jews and against such staunch Nazi political opponents as Socialists and Communists. In 1931 alone, they desecrated 50 synagogues and defiled more than 100 Jewish cemeteries. Now swollen to a private army of more than 400,000 and buoyed by Hitler's rise to power, the Storm Troopers escalated the local *Einzeloperationen*, or individual operations. There were so many beatings, murders, lootings of Jewish businesses, and humiliations—such as forcing Jews to disrobe in public—that Hitler himself grew alarmed. This undirected terror and intimidation threatened the support of the traditional power brokers, such as the industrialists and army generals, whom he needed in his drive toward absolute authority.

In order to channel the destructive energies of the Storm Troopers and also to exert economic pressure, Hitler borrowed a weapon that the Brownshirts already had tried at the local level: the boycott of Jewish-owned businesses. Hitler decided that the Nazi party should conduct such a boycott on a nationwide scale. He appointed a committee of fourteen party leaders headed by Julius Streicher, the most notorious anti-Semite among the early Nazis. Streicher was the party gauleiter, or leader, of Franconia and publisher of *Der Stürmer*, the weekly newspaper whose sex-obsessed ravings against the Jews bordered on the pornographic. The boycott on April 1, 1933, was enforced by the Storm Troopers, who stood with arms linked in front of tens of thousands of Jewish shops, offices, and retail businesses. The doors and windows were painted in yellow on black with the six-pointed Star of David and plastered with signs warning customers away from the premises.

The boycott was frightening but generally ineffective. Streicher and the organizers had selected a Saturday, when a number of stores were closed anyway for the Jewish Sabbath. Many Germans simply ignored the Brownshirts and went on shopping in their favorite stores. International protests and threats of a counterboycott of German goods from the United States and England forced Hitler to limit the boycott to one day. Still, many Jews were stunned "that this cultured German nation," as Zionist leader Benno Cohn said later, "would resort to such iniquitous things."

On April 7, less than a week after the boycott, Hitler launched a legislative assault on the Jews. He approved decrees banning almost all persons of non-Aryan descent from civil service and from the practice of law. In quick order, he promulgated additional laws that prevented non-Aryan physicians from affiliating with health-service institutions and limited the numbers of Jews who could be admitted to high schools and universities. On September 29, he excluded them from farming, which affected few Jews directly; on the same day, however, he ruined thousands of Jewish careers by establishing the Reich Chambers of Culture. This legislation instituted mandatory guilds for employees in the fields of film, theater, music, the fine arts, and journalism under the control of Propaganda Minister Joseph Goebbels—who forbade Jews from joining the guilds and, thus, from working. A new conscription law preventing Jews from serving in the military completed for all practical purposes the official exclusion of Jews from public life.

The legal attack, made up of some 400 anti-Jewish laws that were handed down between 1933 and 1939, reached its peak in 1935. At Hitler's behest, a set of comprehensive new laws was prepared for passage by his rubber-stamp parliament, the Reichstag, meeting in special session on September 15 at the annual party rally in Nuremberg. The legislation, subsequently referred to as the Nuremberg Laws, isolated the Jew legally, politically, and socially. One law restricted citizenship to those of "German or kindred blood" and thus stripped the Jews of those few shreds of political rights that remained for German citizens. Another decree, grandly named the Law for the Protection of German Blood and German Honor, prohibited marriage and extramarital sexual intercourse between Jews and Germans. Presumably to reduce opportunities for the latter, the law forbade the employment in Jewish households of German housemaids under the age of forty-five.

Humiliated by his SA keepers, a Jewish lawyer in Nuremberg carries a sign reading, "I shamed a Christian girl." The Nuremberg Laws established by the Nazis in September 1935 forbade marriage or sexual intercourse between Jews and Germans.

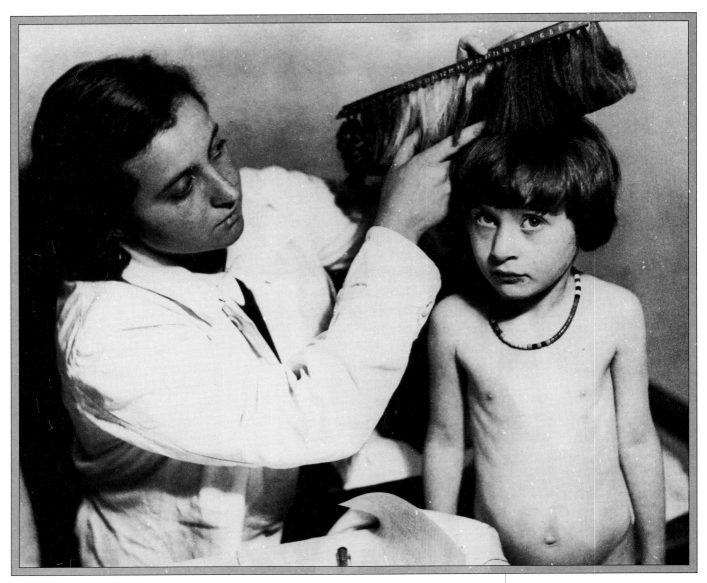

The new laws, as approved at Nuremberg, did not yet provide a definition of the Jew who was being so cruelly segregated by the Third Reich. This problem of definition had plagued Nazi racial ideologists all along. To their embarrassment, none of the party research institutes devoted to investigation of Jewish matters ever succeeded in pinpointing a particular Jewish blood type, physical characteristic, or other biological evidence of race. As a result, Nazi definitions of Jewishness had resorted to the old criterion, religion. Under previous laws, the condition of having at least one grandparent who practiced Judaism was sufficient to define a Jew, regardless of that person's own religious preference.

To enforce the Nuremberg legislation, however, Hitler wanted to settle the question once and for all. He ordered the Interior Ministry's racial experts to help draft the laws and to define the people they were designed to punish. One of these experts was Bernard Lösener, a former customs administration bureaucrat who was called to serve in the Nazi party as a racial specialist in 1933 but had long since become covertly disaffected. Lösener was now playing a dangerous game, trying to help ameliorate the lot of the Jews while maintaining the appearance of being a good Nazi. Hoping to lessen the impact of the Nuremberg Laws, he did his best to limit

A technician with the Reich Office for Research on Race Hygiene and Population Biology in Berlin compares a girl's hair with tinted fiberglass samples. The Nazi obsession with racial purity led to the creation of research institutes that conducted pseudoscientific tests to determine an individual's racial and ethnic background.

the number of people to whom they would apply. In one of his drafts, for example, he boldly inserted the sentence, "This law applies only to full-blooded Jews." At the last minute, Hitler penciled out the sentence.

Working out the final definition of what constituted a Jew required approximately eight weeks of tortured debate after the passage of the Nuremberg Laws. Lösener and his colleagues in the Interior Ministry met seven days a week with functionaries from the party. These Nazi officials, led by Dr. Gerhard Wagner, the party's viciously anti-Semitic medical leader, wanted to classify as a Jew a person who was only one-eighth Jewish. Lösener countered that such a person was actually seven-eighths German. By the same token, Lösener argued that half-Jews (two Jewish grandparents) were also half-German.

Lösener achieved surprising success in the bureaucratic infighting. The first of the supplementary decrees to the Nuremberg Laws, published on November 14, 1935, indicated that he had failed in one major battle: Anyone with at least three Jewish grandparents was deemed a Jew. But the remaining definitions followed Lösener's reasoning. Those with two Jewish grandparents were to be counted as Jews if they belonged to the Jewish religion or were married to a Jew. Half-Jews and one-fourth Jews—those descended from one Jewish grandparent—who did not practice Judaism were lumped together in a new non-Aryan racial category created by the decree—Mischlinge (mixed race).

In effect, Lösener had arbitrarily created a third race, neither German nor Jewish. By the estimate of one Nazi official, some 300,000 persons were half- or one-fourth Jews in the Mischlinge category and thus exempt from the Nuremberg Laws. While escaping the worst measures directed against Jews, they would have to shoulder increasingly harsh burdens imposed explicitly upon their "race." The complex racial definitions now attached to the Nuremberg Laws rendered proof of ancestry more important than ever in the Reich. The genealogical researchers known as Sippenforscher, who helped clients produce the necessary birth certificates and other legal documents to establish their racial purity, developed a thriving business.

Nazi racial obsessions, while focusing most passionately on the Jews, also engulfed Germany's estimated 20,000 Gypsies. The ideologists deemed them a separate and inferior race of "alien" blood. Like the Jews, they had been excluded as non-Aryans from the civil service and armed forces and subjected to the miscegenation clauses of the Nuremberg Laws. Later, Gypsies would be required to register with the police under a law labeled Fight Against the Gypsy Menace. Relying on the Gypsies' old reputation for petty thievery, the authorities also used vaguely worded laws dealing with habitual criminals and asocial elements to harass them. Hundreds of

Gypsies were imprisoned in the Reich's growing complex of concentration camps, there to suffer brutal maltreatment in the company of socialists, communists, dissident churchmen, and homosexuals.

For a time, the Nazi regime deliberately soft-pedaled the Nuremberg Laws and other anti-Jewish measures. Hitler wanted to refrain from actions that might disrupt the Reich's economic recovery from the Great Depression. And he wanted to appease the international community to eliminate the possibility that the 1936 Olympic Games might be shifted from Berlin to another location. The presence of the Olympics and the platoons of foreign visitors whom Hitler tried to please prolonged the period of relative quiet on the racial front.

This ebb in persecution led Jews to hope that the worst had passed. Many rationalized that at least the Nuremberg Laws might have stabilized their status in the new German society, albeit as less than second-class citizens. Remarkably, some of the more than 75,000 German Jews who had fled the country during the first three years of Nazi rule began to return. Many of them banked on their faith that most Germans were sympathetic to their plight. In August 1937, the Zionist leader Arthur Ruppin noted in his diary the hopeful view of a colleague, Rabbi Leo Baeck: "He believes that 80 percent of the German people are against the persecution of the Jews, but they do not dare voice their opinion."

Whatever the accuracy of that assessment, the campaign against the Jews was already escalating again on all fronts—and with scarcely a German Christian voice raised against it. Economic pressure had been building steadily all along. A government boycott, for example, had been instituted in 1935, forbidding public agencies and their employees to patronize Jewish firms. The boycott also applied to Nazi party members, and even the smallest transgression sometimes brought harsh punishment. A Nazi named Kurt Prelle was expelled from the party and prevented from practicing his profession as a notary; his wife, without his knowledge, had committed the offense of purchasing ten pfennig worth of picture postcards in a Jewish-owned store.

Taking away Jewish-owned businesses was the obvious next step. In late 1937, the pressure to expropriate property began to mount. Hitler's new economics czar, Hermann Göring, chief of the Four-Year Plan, stepped up the program known as Aryanization, a euphemism for the seizure of Jewish enterprises by Germans.

A series of government decrees the following year facilitated the takeover process. The Interior Ministry broadened the definition of targets to encompass any business "predominately under Jewish influence." This included businesses with even a a single Jew on the board of directors or even a Jewish legal representative. All Jews with property worth more than 5,000 marks had to register with the government. Aryanization, which had hitherto been voluntary—leaving at least some room for price negotiation between Jewish owners and the new buyers—became compulsory. Other decrees simply shut down a wide variety of Jewish shops, businesses, and services, including the professional practices of physicians. These measures proved so devastating that of the 39,552 businesses still owned by Jews on April 1, 1938, only about 20 percent eluded liquidation or Aryanization during the following year.

While the Nazi regime visited this fast-growing economic destruction on the Jews during 1938, the party's street thugs revived an old, familiar kind of violence. Public terror and physical intimidation escalated, finally erupting that autumn in the cascade of hate and destruction that Nazis would refer to mockingly by the poetic name *Kristallnacht*—the Night of Broken Glass. The worst outbreak of anti-Semitic savagery since the pogroms in Russia during the late nineteenth century, Kristallnacht was the result of a recent outrage against the Jews. In March 1938, the government of Poland, which was presiding over its own epidemic of anti-Semitic violence, had threatened to revoke the citizenship of 70,000 Polish Jews, some of whom had been living in Germany for decades.

In early October, Hitler, afraid of being saddled with a stateless community, ordered these Polish Jews forcibly expelled to their homeland. In the Reich's first experiment with mass deportation, the police rounded up the Polish Jews on October 27, crammed them into railroad cars, and dumped them at the Polish border. Under the muzzles of Polish machine guns, more than 17,000 crossed over from the adopted land that no longer wanted them into a hostile reception from their native country. Less than a fortnight later, on November 7, Herschel Grynszpan, whose parents had been subjected to this cruel indignity, took his revenge. He walked into the German embassy in Paris and fired two shots into Ernst vom Rath, the third secretary. Mortally wounded, the diplomat died two days later.

The death of this minor foreign service officer coincided with the annual Nazi celebration commemorating the Munich Beer Hall Putsch of 1923. Party radicals, including the Storm Troopers, whose power had been broken by Hitler in 1934, seized upon the incident as an excuse to unleash their pent-up fury against the Jews. The primary instigator of the violence was Propaganda Minister Joseph Goebbels, who was attempting to get back into Hitler's good graces after a scandalous affair with Czech film star Lida Baarova. He made certain that the state-controlled press waxed indignant over the obscure diplomat's death, and he then won Hitler's approval to

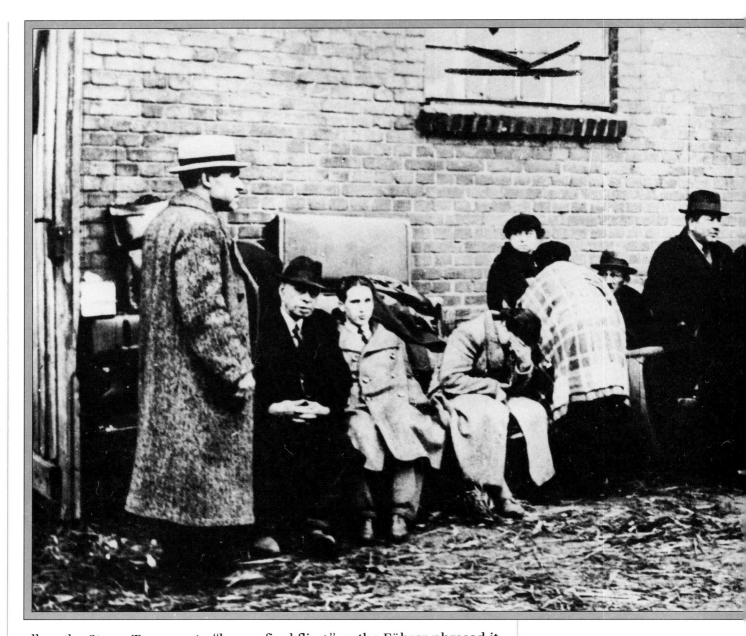

allow the Storm Troopers to "have a final fling," as the Führer phrased it.

The orders went out, and all over the Reich on the night of November 9, the Storm Troopers took to the streets crying for vengeance. The Brownshirts invaded synagogues and Jewish homes and shops to break and burn and loot. Their wake was paved with the shards of glass from the shattered windows that gave Kristallnacht its name. Roving gangs set fire to nearly 200 synagogues and wrecked others with axes and sledgehammers. They built bonfires of prayer books, Torah scrolls, and precious volumes of history and philosophy. They threw Jews from upper-floor windows, shot them, stomped them with their feet, mauled them with fists and truncheons. Nearly 100 of their victims died.

The savage scope of the violence stunned Heinrich Himmler, the SS leader and police chief, who had not been alerted beforehand. During the night, he sent last-minute orders to the Gestapo to prevent large-scale looting—while proceeding with the mass arrest of Jews. Some 30,000 men—nearly 1 in every 10 Jews who had remained in the Reich—were rounded up and interned in concentration camps such as Dachau, outside

In October 1938, Polish Jews expelled from Germany anxiously await their fate in the border town of Zbaszyn. That month, the Nazis rounded up Jews of Polish descent from all over Germany, herded them onto trains, and shipped them east to Poland. Those Jews abandoned at Zbaszyn eventually found shelter at an old military base.

Munich, that had been built to terrorize political adversaries and others deemed enemies of the state. Brutality in the camps during the weeks following Kristallnacht claimed several hundred additional lives.

A few priests, ministers, and others spoke out in protest. A week after Kristallnacht, in the tiny parish of Oberlennigen in southwestern Germany, a Protestant minister named Julius von Jan denounced the pogrom from his pulpit and called for contrition and remorse. A Nazi mob later dragged Pastor Jan from his Bible class, beat him, and smashed his parsonage. The authorities then sent him to a concentration camp.

More remarkable were the mutterings of distress heard at the highest levels of the Nazi regime. Himmler, who objected to the inefficiency of uncontrolled violence, attributed the pogrom to Goebbels's "lust for power." Göring was disturbed by the potential economic disruptions. He feared that the shock waves abroad might result in boycotts of German exports, and he was concerned that the destruction of all that Jewish property—with an estimated total damage of 25 million marks, more than one-fourth of it in glass windows—might hurt the German insurance companies more than it harmed the Jews. "It is insane to clear out and burn a Jewish warehouse," he pointed out, "then have a German insurance company make good the loss." The decision to fine the Jews of Germany one billion marks as punishment for the vom Rath assassination—to be deducted from insurance payments—partially assuaged Göring's concern.

Kristallnacht marked a turning point in the Jewish policies of the Third Reich. It represented a last-ditch effort by the Nazi radicals to gain control, and the debut of the cold-blooded professionals who would deal with the Jewish question in an orderly manner. Soon after Kristallnacht, Hitler forbade Goebbels from meddling in Jewish affairs and asked Göring to take charge of the problem; Göring in turn looked to Himmler's highly efficient SS security apparatus. Under Himmler, the SS had burgeoned from its origin as Hitler's bodyguard into an elite corps of key security organizations such as the Gestapo political police and the party's semiofficial Security Service, the Sicherheitsdienst (SD).

On January 24, 1939, Göring commissioned Reinhard Heydrich, Himmler's deputy, to bring the "Jewish question to as favorable a solution as present circumstances permit." The solution was to be forced emigration. The Jews, having been to a large extent expelled from the economy and most other aspects of German life, were now to be driven from the Reich itself. Germany was to be *Judenrein*, or Jew free.

The SS had been proposing massive emigration as a solution to the so-called Jewish problem since 1934. The central figure in many of the emigration schemes was Adolf Eichmann, a meek-looking bureaucrat who would come to embody the cold impersonality of the Nazi killing machine. Though a native of the Rhineland, Eichmann grew up in Austria in a middle-class family, the son of an accountant and coal-mining entrepreneur. An indifferent student, Eichmann dropped out of a technical high school and eventually became a traveling salesman for a company that distributed oil products. He returned to Germany in 1933, after Hitler took power, and joined the SS. The following year, he found a clerical job in the SD, the new intelligence branch headed by Heydrich. He quickly demonstrated a bent for the intricacies of the bureaucracy and a knack for heel-clicking subservience to senior officers.

Women gather before the shattered windows of a Jewish shop in Berlin after the pogrom of November 9, 1938, a night of violence that erupted after a Jew shot and killed a minor German diplomat in Paris. Propaganda Minister Joseph Goebbels declared, "The natural and fully justified outrage felt by the German people has been expressed this evening."

On November 10, 1938, SS men force Jews to march through the resort town of Baden-Baden carrying a Star of David that reads, "God, do not abandon us." One man seized in the roundup later wrote, "Most of the inhabitants creditably kept out of sight. The spectators who did turn out were of the basest kind."

Eichmann also developed an interest in Jews. Since he was not known to be particularly anti-Semitic, and had a Jewish mistress as well, he may have simply seen an opportunity for advancement in a Nazi organization that loathed Jews but knew very little about them. He was transferred to the SD bureau that was concerned with Jewish affairs—Section II 112. He learned a smattering of Yiddish and Hebrew and suddenly found himself acknowledged as an expert. Among his accomplishments, he proclaimed later, was the determination that the "Führer's diet cook, who was at one time his mistress, was 1/32d Jewish," a finding immediately classified top-secret by his superior.

Such industry brought Eichmann promotion in 1937 as the bureau's chief of Jewish emigration. By that time, Himmler had concluded that massive resettlement was the solution to the Jewish question, and Palestine an attractive receiving ground. The British, in the Balfour Declaration of 1917, had promised to create in Palestine a "national home for the Jewish people." The SS officially encouraged Zionist activities in Germany aimed at promoting resettlement in the British mandate. Some 8,000 German Jews emigrated there annually during the mid-1930s. To explore possibilities of stepping up the flow, Eichmann met in Berlin with a representative of the Haganah—the Jewish military underground in Palestine—and even made a trip there. More than two decades after his trip to Palestine, Eichmann expressed a profound admiration for the Jewish colonists' "desperate will to live, the more so since I was myself an idealist." He added, "In the years that followed, I often said to Jews with whom I had dealings that had I been a Jew, I would have been a fanatical Zionist."

As it turned out, Palestine proved to be no panacea for Eichmann and other Nazi enthusiasts of mass emigration. Many German Jews lacked the pioneering skills and the desire required to carve a new life out of the desert. The British, faced with heightened hostility between Jew and Arab, severely limited immigration to Palestine. Hitler, for his part, had second thoughts about contributing to the creation of an independent state comprising his mortal enemies. Fearing that it "might become the spiritual center for the international Jewish conspiracy," he ordered suspension of further negotiations for large-scale transfer of Jews to Palestine. Emigration of Germans Jews declined sharply.

But Eichmann was making his mark nonetheless. Promoted to the rank of lieutenant in the SS, he was sent on an important mission to Vienna in 1938. The annexation of Austria had brought 200,000 additional Jews into the Reich, and Eichmann's job was to force them to emigrate. In Vienna's old Rothschild mansion, he established the Central Office of Jewish Emigration, bringing together under one roof representatives of all the government agencies involved in the emigration process. "It should be a conveyor belt," said Eichmann. "You put the first document followed by the other papers in at one end, and out comes the passport at the other." This assembly-line technique, which typically allowed an applicant to complete in one day what required weeks in Germany itself, was soon processing papers for as many as 1,000 émigrés daily.

Besides streamlining emigration, Eichmann introduced other innovations in Vienna. He pressured wealthy Jews to subsidize the emigration of poorer ones. And he sent Jewish emissaries abroad not only to raise funds but also to procure the foreign currency necessary for an emigrant's entrance into another country. By running roughshod over normal emigration procedures, Eichmann developed a program of forced deportation that did not even guarantee acceptance at the other end. It led to highly publicized international incidents of ships carrying Jewish refugees shuttling from port to port seeking permission to disgorge their human cargo. Jews from Austria wound up in such faraway places as Shanghai. But what impressed Berlin was numbers: Eichmann succeeded in shipping out 50,000 Austrian Jews in half a year, while Germany, using standard emigration procedures, accounted for only 19,000.

Eichmann's operation was considered such a success that it was copied in Germany. When Göring commissioned Heydrich to solve the Jewish question through resettlement in January 1939, he specifically ordered the establishment of a Reich Central Office of Jewish Emigration based on the Eichmann model. But the new agency faced greater obstacles than those confronting Eichmann in Vienna. About 150,000 German Jews had emigrated since the Nazis came to power in 1933, but the yearly totals now showed a steady decline. Because of age or lack of wealth or skills, the 350,000 Jews still in Germany tended to be less likely to seek or find refuge

Adolf Eichmann, who arranged the deportation of Jews throughout Europe to Nazi extermination camps, prided himself on being a good family man. His favorite photo was one taken with his bride on their wedding day in 1935 *(top left)*. Posing as a journalist *(top right)*, he visited Palestine in 1937 to explore the possibility of deporting Jews to that nation. After arriving in Austria in March 1938 to organize the expulsion of Jews, he participated in a raid on a Jewish community office in Vienna *(bottom, third from right)*.

abroad. More than half of them were over forty-five years of age, and nearly one-fifth were older than sixty-five.

The most formidable bars to large-scale emigration, however, were the policies of other nations. The rising tide of anti-Semitism, spilling over from Poland, Hungary, Rumania, and other eastern European nations as well as from Germany, had created a worldwide glut of refugees—and a sharply reduced willingness to take them in. From Poland alone, more than 400,000 Jews had emigrated in less than two decades. In June 1939, a few months after establishment of the Reich Central Office, the SD reported a "growing tendency for other countries to lock their doors against immigration."

The hardening response to Jewish refugees had been illustrated the previous summer when the American president, Franklin D. Roosevelt, called for an international conference on the problem. Representatives of thirty-two countries met in July 1938 at the French resort town of Évian. Not all of the delegates were immune to the virus of racism that had created the problem in the first place. "It will no doubt be appreciated," the delegate from Australia announced, "that as we have no racial problem, we are not desirous of importing one." The Évian conference accomplished little. In its aftermath, even normally receptive countries like the United States and Britain, both of which had accepted large numbers of Jewish immigrants, tightened their rules of admission.

During this period, high-level negotiations aimed at getting neighboring countries to accept German Jews were carried on by Foreign Minister Joachim von Ribbentrop. In December 1938, five months after the Évian conference, Ribbentrop talked with Georges-Étienne Bonnet, foreign minister of France, a country that traditionally had provided asylum for refugees of all sorts. According to Ribbentrop's notes of the meeting, Bonnet not only refused to accept any more Jews from Germany but also wanted to ship 10,000 Jews already in France "somewhere else." Ribbentrop wrote that he had told Bonnet that "we all wanted to get rid of our Jews but that the difficulties lay in the fact that no country wished to receive them."

Despite these obstacles, the Reich Central Office succeeded in nearly doubling the rate of emigration during 1939. About 78,000 Jews left Germany that year, primarily as a result of high-pressure tactics. Jewish agencies in Berlin were forced to submit a daily list of seventy families prepared to emigrate. Among those who departed were several thousand people smuggled by ship into Palestine past a blockade of British destroyers. Their success was the result of a secret collaborative effort between Zionists and the SD. Meanwhile, Eichmann, newly promoted to captain, set up shop in Prague soon after the German conquest of Czechoslovakia in March 1939 and quickly processed the emigration of more than 30,000 local Jews.

A German Orthodox Jew emigrating from his homeland to Rio de Janeiro, Brazil, prays aboard a ship during the transatlantic passage in 1938. When nations such as the United States and Great Britain refused to accept the refugees, Hitler observed, "The entire democratic world dissolves in tears of pity but then closes its heart to the poor, tortured Jewish people."

Forced emigration remained the priority of the Nazi regime even with the outbreak of war on September 1, 1939, when Hitler invaded Poland. The peripatetic Eichmann returned to Berlin the following month to take over as director of the Reich Central Office. His problems were now compounded by the presence of so many Jews in Poland. Ten percent of Poland's prewar population of 33 million was Jewish, representing the the largest group of Jews in Europe. After the dismemberment of Poland, about 2 million of them resided in the German-occupied zone; the remainder lived in the eastern zone occupied by the Soviet Union. By mid-1940, Eichmann was feverishly at work on the most ambitious emigration scheme of all, a plan designed to accommodate some 4 million European Jews.

The so-called Madagascar Plan was proposed by the German Foreign Office after the defeat of France in June 1940. The idea of deporting Jews to the French colony of Madagascar, a large island off the southeast coast of Africa, actually dated back nearly a century and a half to the time of Napoleon. More recently, in 1937, the Polish regime had looked into the possibility of relocating its Jews there. According to the new scheme devised by the German Foreign Office, France would cede the island to Germany. The German navy would have its choice of bases there, and the remainder of the 228,000-square-mile island would become a reservation for Jews under the overall jurisdiction of Himmler and the SS. The presence of the black-shirted police would make possible an added advantage of the Madagascar Plan: The Jews could be held hostage there to influence the policies of the United States.

Eichmann, who envisioned himself as governor of this new Jewish state, enthusiastically began to develop detailed blueprints. He even commissioned legal experts to draft laws to cover the plan. But the scheme hinged on the conclusion of a peace treaty with France, which in turn depended on an end of hostilities with England. The British Royal Navy, in any event, controlled the sea lanes necessary for the transport of all those people.

While Eichmann was laboring at this plan, which was the last major effort to solve the Jewish problem by means of emigration, the machinery of a new solution already was in motion. Hundreds of thousands of Jews—mostly Poles but also Germans, Austrians, Czechs, and Slovaks—were being uprooted from their homes, transported eastward, and concentrated in urban ghettos in Poland.

Reinhard Heydrich launched this new phase of evacuation and concentration on September 21, 1939, three weeks after Germany invaded Poland. He told a meeting of his department heads in the Reich Central Security Office (RSHA), an organization headed by Heydrich and encom-

By July 1942, Adolf Hitler's persecution of Jews, Gypsies, and other undesirables had taken the form of a network of ghettos, labor camps, and killing camps throughout the region the Nazis called Greater Germany *(pale green)*. The first labor camp opened in 1933 at Dachau near Munich. By 1939, six camps held 25,000 prisoners. Between 1939 and 1941, the policy of isolating and deporting Jews and others shifted to one of annihilating them. In 1942, the Nazis opened Belzec, Sobibor, and Treblinka, three killing camps equipped with gas chambers, for the sole purpose of murdering Poland's Jews. Installations such as Majdanek and Chelmno, originally labor camps, were eventually used for killing. Auschwitz was both a labor camp and a killing camp, containing barracks for prisoners and gas chambers for those too weak or too ill to work. In 1942, the Nazis chose it as the primary execution site for the Jews from western Europe.

passing the Gestapo, SS, SD, and Criminal Police, that these measures were the "first steps in the final solution." His phrase, *die Endlösung*—the final solution—had not yet acquired its horrendous meaning. It had been first used the year before by Wilhelm Stuckart, one of the authors of the Nuremberg Laws, to indicate that legislation was only a stopgap measure until the Jews were driven from Germany, and evidently did not yet imply mass murder. Heydrich's first steps of evacuation and concentration were tied to the new territorial boundaries that were about to be imposed on the defeated Poles. The Reich simply annexed the northern and western portions of German-occupied Poland, including provinces that Germany had given up in the Versailles treaty after World War I. The southern and eastern rump of the dismembered enemy nation became an occupation zone, in effect a German colony designated the Government General of Poland. One million Jews—600,000 from the annexed regions and 400,000 from the Reich—were to be dumped into the Government General, along with many thousands of unwanted Gypsies and Polish gentiles. These mass movements were designed to make room in the annexed area for the Ethnic Germans who were moving westward, under special agreement with the

Russians, from the Baltic States and other regions under Soviet rule.

The trains began to roll on December 1, 1939. So many Jews, Poles, and Gypsies were poured into the Government General—an average of 3,000 a day—that they overwhelmed the capabilities of the new administration, which already had 1.4 million Jews under its jurisdiction. In February 1940, the powerful and vain governor, Hans Frank, who was engaged in a power struggle with Himmler for control of policy in his territory, protested to Göring. A month later, after some 200,000 people had been deposited in the Government General, Göring ordered an end to all evacuations except those that were approved by Frank.

In the meantime, the process of concentrating and isolating the Jews got under way throughout Poland. To a great extent—although it had occurred without careful design—this process had already been carried out in Germany. The 215,000 Jews who remained there at the outbreak of the war lived in ghettos without walls. More than two-thirds of them resided in a few large cities, clustered together for mutual support.

The many ghettos created by the Nazi masters of Poland not only telescoped the deprivations in the Reich, they went far beyond them. In November 1939, for example, Jews in the Government General of Poland were forced to wear special insignia—a white armband with a blue, six-pointed Star of David—nearly two years before wearing the yellow star on a black background became mandatory for their fellow Jews in Germany.

Most of the new ghettos in Poland maintained the prisonlike atmosphere of their medieval predecessors. Frequently surrounded by barbed wire, they effectively isolated the Jews from the outside world. In some instances, a formidable masonry wall enclosed the ghetto; in Krakow, the wall was constructed in the form of Jewish tombstones as if to remind the inhabitants that they were buried alive. Passage in and out of most ghettos was strictly controlled, and movement inside was usually limited to the daylight hours. The location typically was the dirtiest, poorest, and most crowded section of the city. In Warsaw, the prewar capital, more than 400,000 inhabitants were crammed into the largest of the Polish ghettos, averaging more than a half-dozen per room. "A race of lower standing needs less room," explained one of Hitler's longtime cronies, Robert Ley, "less clothing, less food, and less culture than a race of higher standing."

Jews were forced to wear a Star of David emblem, which they made from different materials and displayed in various ways. In Bulgaria, star-shape yellow-and-black buttons were sewn onto clothing *(top)*. In the Netherlands, France, and Germany, yellow cloth badges inscribed with the word *Jew* were used, while Jews in the Warsaw ghetto tied on armbands *(fourth from top)*. Those who refused to wear a star faced a fine or imprisonment.

The Nazi overseers imposed the onus of administering the day-to-day affairs of the ghettos on the Jews themselves. Each ghetto was governed by a *Judenrat*, or Jewish Council, appointed by the Germans or elected by the residents. The chairman of the council served in effect as mayor, sometimes with extraordinary powers. The 200,000 Jews in the ghetto in Lodz were ruled in autocratic fashion by the council chairman, Chaim Rumkowski. The former head of a Jewish orphanage, Rumkowski was about seventy years old. With his flowing mane of white hair and cloak, he made his regal way about the streets of the ghetto in a broken-down horse carriage provided by the Germans. The eccentric patriarch issued currency with his signature and had postage stamps printed bearing his likeness. "He considers himself God's anointed," noted Emanuel Ringelblum, chronicler of the Warsaw ghetto, in his diary.

It was the tragic fate of the Jewish Council in every ghetto to preside over appalling deprivation. The Judenrat recruited workers on demand under

Jewish youngsters toil in a locksmith's workroom in Lodz, Poland, to fill contracts for the German army in 1942. Beginning in 1939, the Germans segregated the Jews of Poland in ghettos and forced those over the age of twelve to work in labor camps.

the German policy of forced labor—for cooperative workshops and private enterprise within the ghetto, for labor battalions to clean the streets of the entire city, and for the labor camps, where Jews worked to the point of collapse digging canals or building military fortifications. The Judenrat doled out the meager food that was supplied bv the Germans; in Warsaw, the typical ghetto allocation eventually fell below 300 calories a day. Council members also had to cope with epidemics of typhus, tuberculosis, and other diseases that flourished among ill-fed, ill-clad people forced to exist jammed together in filth.

The toll was predictable. By early 1941, Jews in Warsaw were dying of

Jewish police appointed to keep order in the Warsaw ghetto hurry down a street in their jurisdiction. The Germans recruited Jews to maintain order in all Polish ghettos.

A German guard seizes a Jewish boy trying to smuggle food into the Warsaw ghetto. Children often slipped out of the ghetto and scavenged for food to sell inside on the black market.

starvation at a rate of more than 2,000 a month. In all, 44,360 residents died that year of all causes, more than 10 percent of the ghetto population. "Death lies in every street," wrote Ringelblum on May 11, 1941. "The children are no longer afraid of death. In one courtyard, the children played a game of tickling a corpse."

Although the policy of confining the Jews to ghettos could be regarded as a major step toward their gradual extermination through hunger, disease, and forced labor, Hans Frank and other Nazi administrators in Poland viewed the situation differently. Especially during the early stages, they spoke of concentration as a transitional phase and still endorsed the possibility of mass emigration to Madagascar as the preferred final solution to the Jewish problem.

The Führer, however, had more than once signaled his own intentions. His most ominous warning had come on January 30, 1939, seven months before the war began. "In my life I have often been a prophet, and most of the time I have been laughed at," he told the Reichstag. "During my struggle for power, the Jews laughed at my prophecy that I would someday assume the leadership of the state. I suppose that the laughter of Jewry is now choking in their throats. Today I will be a prophet again. If international Jewry should succeed once more in plunging the peoples into a world war,

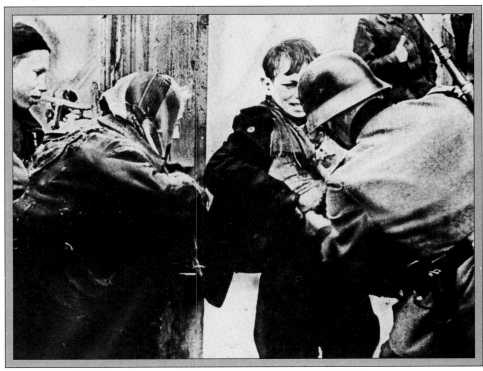

the consequence will not be the Bolshevization of the earth and a victory of Jewry, but on the contrary, the destruction of the Jewish race in Europe."

Soon after the speech, as if in rehearsal for that eventuality, Hitler inaugurated two secret programs of systematic murder. They were carried out under the rubric of euthanasia, or mercy killing. The subjects, not necessarily Jews but people with severe physical or mental problems, were victims of the same warped notions of biological purity that underlay all of Hitler's racial ideas—as early as 1933, sterilization had also been conducted on individuals not considered "pure." The first program, implemented under the formal guise of the Reich Committee for Scientific Research of Hereditary and Severe Constitutional Diseases, singled out deformed or retarded children. An estimated 5,000 such children were put to death during the next five years, usually by lethal injection, at special centers established in twenty-one hospitals throughout the Reich.

Smoke rises from the crematorium of a euthanasia facility in Hadamar, about thirty-five miles northwest of Frankfurt, in 1941. Authorized by Hitler in September of 1939, the euthanasia program was first directed at the handicapped, retarded, and mentally ill. By the summer of 1940, gas chambers like the one at Hadamar were used to kill concentration-camp inmates who were unfit for work.

Hitler's other program of mercy killing proved to be far more ambitious. "To administer to incurably sick persons a mercy death," he authorized the establishment of the National Coordinating Agency for Therapeutic and Medical Establishments in the autumn of 1939, shortly after the invasion of Poland. It bore the code name T-4, for the address of the agency's headquarters, an inconspicuous villa at Tiergartenstrasse no. 4 in a suburb of Berlin. To ensure secrecy and tight control, he reached no further than his private chancellery for a director, selecting Philip Bouhler, the office's soft-faced, forty-year-old chief. Hitler above all was counting on the clamor of war to conceal the program and suppress possible public dissent.

Medical doctors, including Hitler's personal physician, Dr. Karl Brandt, selected the victims from lists submitted by institutions. Those chosen— typically the senile, feeble-minded, or incurably insane—were transported under the auspices of the Charitable Foundation for Institutional Care to one of six killing centers established in abandoned prisons and asylums. In groups of twenty or thirty, dressed in paper smocks, they were ushered into a tiled chamber disguised as a shower room. Carbon monoxide gas piped into the sealed chamber ended their lives; cremation destroyed the evidence. The family received an urn of ashes and a letter of condolence attributing the death to a natural cause, such as pneumonia, and explaining the cremation as a necessary measure due to the danger of contagion.

Despite the elaborate secrecy, details of T-4 seeped out. People read the death notices in the newspapers with skepticism. Residents near the killing centers watched knowingly as the smoke poured from the chimneys of the crematoriums. In Hadamar, near one of the centers, children ran after the buses with the blacked-out windows shouting, "There goes the murder box again." Prominent Catholic and Protestant clerics finally began to attack the program openly from the pulpit. In August 1941, after more than 70,000 victims had experienced the purported mercy of death in the gas chamber, Hitler yielded to public pressure and ordered the termination of T-4. The killing continued in a companion program, code-named 14f13, under which thousands of concentration-camp inmates—political prisoners, habitual criminals, Jews, and others who were too sick to work—were certified as insane and put to death in a T-4 center or the camp's own newly installed gas chamber.

T-4 was history's first laboratory for mass murder. If, as he said, Hitler intended to destroy the Jews rather than merely expel them through laws, forced emigration, or evacuation into ghettos, the apparatus of destruction was taking shape. The executioners were trained, the technology proved, the procedures worked out. Gas-chamber crews had even learned to turn a profit for the Reich by extracting gold-filled teeth from the corpses. ✚

A Plan for Persecuting Gypsies

In their mania for what they termed racial purity and their loathing of non-Aryans, the Nazis ranked Europe's Gypsy peoples with the Jews as special targets for persecution, exile, imprisonment—and eventual extermination. The Gypsies, wanderers who originated in ancient India and who had maintained their ethnic uniqueness over centuries of living among Europeans, invoked Nazi hatred because of their perceived "Asian" features, their swarthy skins, their itinerant lifestyle, and their separateness. Above all, they were seen as threatening the pure blood of the German race as a result of intermarriage. In German eyes, they were Untermenschen, who, like the Jews, were fit only to be isolated, hemmed in, got rid of.

Nazi officials and pseudoexperts on race tried, as they did with the Jews, to legitimize these prejudices and the persecutions that grew out of them by accumulating scientific proof of the Gypsies' inferiority. Leading the effort was psychiatrist Robert Ritter, head of the Reich Office for Research on Race Hygiene and Population Biology. Ritter dispatched researchers to take a census of Germany's Gypsies, assembling complex genealogies and cataloging degrees of mixed German-Gypsy blood among many of them. He and his assistants examined and tested hundreds of Gypsies—as shown in the photographs on these and the following pages. Ritter reported that they were a "people of entirely primitive ethnological origins" who formed a "criminal asocial subproletariat." He concluded that Gypsies should be "collected in large camps and set to work" or, better yet, be eliminated altogether.

A roundup of the Gypsies began in 1940 with the deportation shown on pages 44-47. These victims were the first of many thousands from Germany and from the Nazi-occupied nations of Europe, most of whom either were slaughtered or ultimately died of abuse or starvation in concentration camps. In all, between 250,000 and 500,000 Gypsies perished.

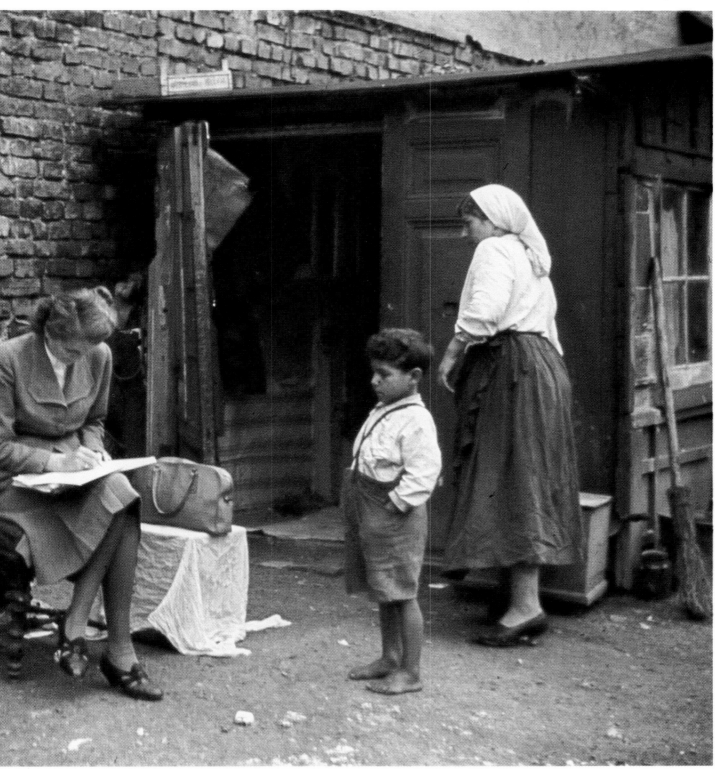

Eva Justin, Robert Ritter's chief assistant, takes notes during an interview of a Gypsy family in the courtyard of an urban slum. Some Gypsies had given up their wandering life to live in towns, but like their itinerant fellows, most of them remained poor.

Measuring for Marks of Inferiority

Spurred on by a 1938 law that decreed the registration of all Gypsies, Ritter and his cohorts redoubled their efforts to track down all of Germany's Gypsies—eventually amassing genealogical files on about 30,000—and subjected increasing numbers of them to blood tests and examinations of eye color, skin pigmentation, and cranial shape. Although Ritter's researchers were not part of the official SS machinery of racial persecution, the Gypsies were forced by local police to submit to their humiliating, frightening tests. Anyone who resisted was threatened with being arrested and sent to a concentration camp. By the same means, Ritter forced a number of Gypsy men and women to undergo surgical sterilization, which rendered them, as one official report phrased it, "biologically harmless."

Pseudoscientific experiments conducted by Ritter to "prove" that Gypsies were by nature social deviants and criminals gave the Nazis a justification for including the Gypsies with the Jews in the final solution. Ritter was indicted after the war for crimes against humanity but never tried. He died in 1951.

At a Gypsy camp, a smiling Dr. Ritter draws a blood sample from the arm of a fearful woman, as a colleague assists and the woman's husband looks on.

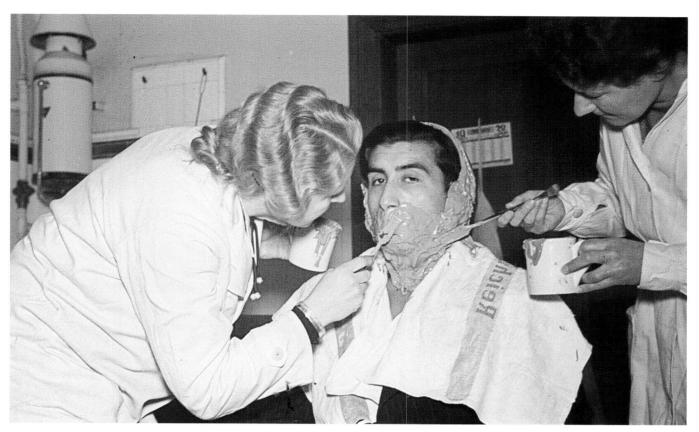

Another member of Ritter's group, Dr. Sophie Ehrhardt, and an assistant *(above)* apply soft wax to a Gypsy's face, making one of a number of life masks used to study Gypsy features.

Dr. Ehrhardt matches a Gypsy woman's eye color with samples on a chart. These and other spurious tests were conducted to demonstrate the "Asian backwardness" of the Gypsies.

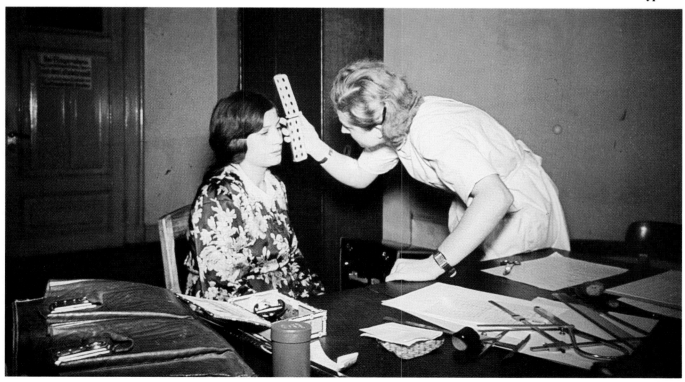

Gypsies gather in a yard of Hohenasperg prison *(above)* in Asperg, a village outside the town of Ludwigsburg, near Stuttgart. Allowed only hand luggage and a musical instrument or two, the deportees wore their best clothes—traditional long skirts, shawls, and head scarves for the women, suits and fedoras for the men. Appearing bewildered by the sudden upheaval in their lives, Gypsy families in the prison courtyard *(right)* huddle together under the guard of civilian police armed with rifles.

The First Deportations

The initial deportations began on May 16, 1940, when police wrenched Gypsies from their homes and places of work and herded them to a series of collection points. Chosen for this first roundup were about 2,800 men, women, and children living in and around various cities in northwestern and western Germany. The Gypsies seen in the photographs here and overleaf were from Mainz, Worms, and Ingelheim; they were assembled at a forbidding 160-year-old prison called Hohenasperg. Their destination was Poland, already the Nazis' chosen dumping ground for undesirables.

At Hohenasperg, the Gypsies had identification numbers stamped on their arms and were forced to sign documents saying they would never attempt to return to their German homes. Their guards were ordinary police drawn from the department in Frankfurt. Unlike the deportation and killing of the Jews, which later would be blamed in large part on Hitler, Himmler, and the SS, the persecution of the Gypsies was carried out by ordinary civil officials, regular police, and members of the scientific community.

Entraining for Oblivion

After a few days, the Gypsies who had assembled at Hohenasperg were herded into trains for a long, nightmarish journey to the Government General, part of Nazi-occupied Poland. There, they were pitched out into fields and forced to build their own camp.

No more deportations occurred until late 1941, when new trainloads of Gypsies began to arrive in Poland. Later, Gypsies in the lands conquered by the Nazis were rounded up for slaughter. Many died of starvation and disease before the gas chambers began their work in early 1942. About 20,000 Gypsies were killed at Auschwitz, and many thousands more died at other concentration camps. Roving SS execution squads murdered 35,000 Gypsies in Poland and unknown numbers throughout the Soviet Union. In Yugoslavia, Croatian Catholic terrorists known as Ustashi surpassed even the SS in their anti-Gypsy atrocities. No more than one-fifth of the prewar Gypsy population in Nazi-held territories survived the Holocaust.

Gypsy deportees lean from the windows of railroad coaches waiting at the Asperg station. Not yet truly alarmed, most Gypsies took their uprooting stoically, unaware of what was to come. Later, facing firing squads and gas chambers, many fought their SS killers with their bare hands.

Watched by people of Asperg, a column of the Gypsies from Hohenasperg prison marches past the steep-gabled houses of the village to the railroad station. The prison looms in the distance, on the summit of a hill covered with terraced vineyards.

Sergeant Heinrich Jöst served for several years in German-occupied Poland. In civilian life, he was an innkeeper.

Neighborhood of Despair

When the Warsaw ghetto was sealed on November 16, 1940, its ten-foot walls and guarded gates encased nearly half a million Jews. It was one more step in the Nazi campaign to destroy the Jewish people throughout the Reich and its occupied lands.

Their property confiscated, their identity proclaimed by compulsory armbands, the ghetto residents—almost one-third of the population of Warsaw, in addition to Jews from other parts of Poland—had been forcibly resettled into less than three percent of the city's area. The Germans cynically explained the confinement as a quarantine, to control the spread of typhus and typhoid. These deadly infections had indeed swept Warsaw after its occupation in September 1939, but had subsided. Within the confines of the crowded ghetto, however, the combined effects of wretched sanitation and the almost total deprivation of food, fuel, and medicine soon rekindled the epidemics. During the summer of 1941, disease and starvation killed 15,655 Jews. Others were shot while trying to escape or when caught in the act of smuggling precious goods to their families. The bodies of the dead were often left lying outside the ghetto walls.

Heinrich Jöst, a German army sergeant whose unit was billeted near Warsaw, noticed the corpses and was intrigued. He decided to satisfy his curiosity, and on the afternoon of September 19, 1941, his forty-third birthday, Jöst walked into the ghetto. His entry was strictly against regulations, as was his use of a camera; the army had forbidden "amateur photography" in the area. But he was wearing his Wehrmacht uniform, and no one challenged him.

Sergeant Jöst wandered freely through the neighborhood streets, snapping pictures as he went; the photographs shown here and on the following pages are his. When he joined his friends that evening for a birthday dinner, he discovered that he was unable to eat. He never told them where he had been, however. Jöst simply had his film developed by a Polish druggist, and then for the next forty years, he showed the pictures to no one. "In my letters home," he later recounted, "I did not say anything about what I had seen. I did not want to upset my family. But I thought, 'Good God, what sort of a world is this?'"

Jöst entered the Warsaw ghetto here, at Leszno Street. The sign, in German and Polish, reads: "Plague-infected area; only through traffic allowed." This was gate no. 2 of an ever-decreasing number of entryways.

A carload of German police,
aided by a Polish collaborator
standing on the running board,
guards one of the ghetto's few
thoroughfares. This street had
been left open for Warsaw trolley
traffic; others had long since
been blocked by high walls.

Shoppers look over clothing in
an open-air market, where Jews
sell their possessions to buy
food. The wife of Nazi governor
general Hans Frank was among
the bargain hunters who flocked
to ghetto bazaars like this one.

A vendor offers pickles and bread, which she safeguards behind a barrier of chicken wire. Otherwise, ravenous people would snatch the food and devour it on the spot.

Inside the gate, Jöst was surrounded by malnourished vendors. Since their businesses had been confiscated, many Jews resorted to peddling. Goods were scarce; getting supplies past the guards depended on bribery and smuggling. Many people hawked their last possessions in order to survive. "The ghetto today," wrote one chronicler, "is a concentration camp whose inmates must support themselves."

For those who had money or connections, a few worldly pleasures remained—a handful of restaurants and cafés where starving performers entertained. But most people were destitute.

Curfew restricted everyone to their homes at night. As the war raged on, contact with the outside world became severely restricted. Writing to relatives was forbidden; listening to foreign broadcasts was punishable by death. The only Jews allowed outside the walls were those impressed into labor gangs.

On top of these hardships was the incessant overcrowding. "A sea of thousands of heads floods the entire street from end to end," wrote one ghetto resident. "Pushing one's way through the great throng is like trying to part the waters of the Red Sea."

The sight overwhelmed Sergeant Jöst, prompting him to remark, "I couldn't think where on earth all these people were supposed to go."

Emaciated and exhausted, a woman sells starched white-and-blue Star-of-David armbands. A severe beating was the penalty for a crumpled or dirty armband; death was the price for not wearing one.

A passerby and a Jewish
policeman come to the aid of an
old man who has collapsed.
Starving people, wrote a ghetto
physician, "die during physical
effort, such as searching for
food, and sometimes even with a
piece of bread in their hands."

waiting to pull the undertaker's
wagon on its rounds of the city;
the horses had been confiscated.

Although September 19, 1941, was a chilly day, Jöst noticed that many windows were open. "Apparently," he noted, "the people lived so tightly crowded together that they needed fresh air." With three and four families assigned to each apartment, ghetto Jews commonly slept nine to a room. Thousands of homeless filled the synagogues; others lived in the streets.

Soap was seldom seen inside the ghetto, and cleanliness became impossible. Typhus-carrying lice multiplied, spreading the disease. Immunizing serum was contraband, costly, and scarce. Tuberculosis, influenza, and intestinal diseases also claimed a legion of victims.

Cold and hunger added to the misery. Lumps of coal were so precious they were called "black pearls," and the food ration fell below starvation level. At less than 300 calories per day, a month's allotment provided no more than three days of normal human consumption. Eating became an obsession. "It is common enough for whole families to die on one day," wrote a ghetto diarist. "If this situation continues, the 'Jewish problem' in Warsaw will soon solve itself."

Too weak to walk, a malnourished mother and child ride in a hired rickshaw. Jöst was shocked to find "people working as transportation vehicles," but the work might enable a rickshaw driver to earn the

...hen (far left),
...ruel made
...ovided once
...ple. At near
...refoot child
...valk. "No
...enny," wrote
...because
...andlers
...earts."

...sit up (far left)
...where, Jöst
...vent on by;
...y such
...o beggar
..., he doubted
...e was still
...his picture.

Sprawled on the cold sidewalk, a woman stares vacantly at a passerby. "People dying of hunger didn't ask me for food," Jöst recalled, "because I was in a German army uniform."

A boy pulls a burial cart with a corpse on it. Unlike this body, most of the dead were sent to the cemetery without shrouds, for there was no cloth to spare

The bodies of the Warsaw dead were taken to the Jewish cemetery on wagons, bicycle rickshaws, stretchers, and hand-drawn carts, like the one above. A few families could still afford a proper burial, but most of the corpses were simply dumped on the sidewalk to be collected, naked and anonymous, perhaps veiled by a covering of paper; clothing was deemed too precious to be buried.

Jöst followed a burial cart to the cemetery, but was unprepared for what he saw there. The bodies, dozens more every day, were interred in common graves without ceremony or tombstones. "There is a marked, remarkable indifference to death, which no longer impresses," wrote one ghetto resident. Relentless, numbing death was at the heart of the Nazi plan. Ludwig Fischer, the Nazi governor of the Warsaw district, predicted, "The Jews will die of hunger and privation, and of the Jewish question only a cemetery will remain."

A gravedigger rolls a corpse over the edge of a mass grave to a fellow worker who waits to place it with other bodies. This man, said Jöst, "lays the corpses very neatly next to and atop one another as if in a case. Then he sprinkles each layer with lime."

TWO

"Without Pity or Mercy"

ay 18, 1943, dawned mild and fair in eastern Poland, and most people in the farming village of Szarajowka began their chores early. They had been up for hours when word spread, about 9:00 a.m., that the Germans were encircling the village. During three years of occupation, the villagers had heard enough horror stories to be panicked by the news. Some learned of the ominous German movement early enough to flee out the road west to neighboring Chmielnik—an avenue of escape briefly left open because of the tardy arrival of one SS detachment. But within fifteen minutes, that road was sealed off, too, and Szarajowka was surrounded.

The German force, consisting of SS, regular troops, and the Gestapo, fanned out through the village, methodically gathering up its inhabitants and their possessions. Young men were shot on the spot as they were encountered. The women, children, and old people were herded into the town square. Some villagers wept, a few laughed hysterically. Most stood dazed and silent, watching as soldiers seized livestock and packed household goods onto carts.

About noon, the Nazi commander ordered the crowd divided into small groups and taken into a few of the larger houses and stables. Then the Germans boarded up the windows and doors, piled straw around the buildings, and set them on fire.

The old wooden structures blazed up quickly. The sharp snapping and popping sound of burning wood added to the ear-piercing din of squealing children, the screams of their parents, and the high wails of the elderly. As the Nazis looked on impassively, one building collapsed, and a lone woman crawled free of the wreckage, only to be shot immediately. Then the uniformed men again spread out through the town, pouring gasoline over the remaining buildings and setting them ablaze.

A few townspeople had survived the flames and suffocation by squeezing into the corners of cellars and gulping the air trapped there. Now, under cover of heavy black smoke, they pulled themselves out of the inferno and

Hans Frank, newly appointed governor general of occupied Poland (center), strides down a ruined Warsaw street in September 1939 with his deputy, Artur Seyss-Inquart (left). Frank's order from Hitler was to "finish off the Poles at all costs."

crawled unseen into nearby cornfields. Gradually, the cries of the others died away. When the town was finally silent except for the crackling of the fire, the Nazis left.

Why had a community that had existed for generations been wiped out in just a few hours? Most likely the massacre was an act of reprisal for some real or imagined partisan activity. The cruel mathematics of Nazi rule in Poland decreed the death of 50 to 100 Poles for every German killed by whatever means, a formula that had been faithfully obeyed since the invasion on September 1, 1939.

Whatever the reason, it was immaterial. To a large extent, the fate of Szarajowka and thousands of other obscure peasant communities scattered across the vast expanse of Poland and the European portion of the Soviet Union had been decided decades earlier in the mind of Adolf Hitler.

Throughout his brooding, failure-wracked youth, Hitler found escape from bitter reality in fantasies about conquering space. The sweeping reaches of eastern Europe beckoned him with an almost mystic pull—a siren song that echoed no less loudly in adulthood, when his personal dreams of conquest, combined with his deep-seated racism, were incorporated into Nazi ideology as the concept of Lebensraum—living space. For Hitler, Lebensraum meant a gigantic German empire in the East, a biologically pure, predominately rural society in which there would be no room for the contaminating presence of racially inferior native populations.

In Hitler's view, both the Jews and the Slavs counted as vermin that had to be cleared from prospective German living space. But a critical distinction between the two groups was woven into Nazi doctrine. What Nazi racial theorists liked to call the "eternal Jew" was a creature of mythic dimensions, a wily string puller endowed with satanic guile who was responsible for every contemporary evil from prostitution to capitalism and Marxism. The Slavs—a designation encompassing most of the 100 or so ethnic and national groups residing in the Soviet Union, as well as the Czechs, Poles, Slovenes, Croats, Slovaks, and Serbs—were another matter. To the Nazis, these Untermenschen were primitive, stupid creatures barely one rung above animals on the evolutionary ladder.

These perceptions created a system of priorities that to some extent dictated the way the Nazis eventually treated the two groups. In essence, Jews posed a great danger. They were objects of fear and loathing, to be uprooted and eliminated as quickly as possible by whatever means were available. Slavs, on the other hand, were merely objects of contempt, inconvenient in that they inhabited land coveted by Germany. Otherwise, they were a threat only because their proximity presented the possibility of racial contamination, or insofar as they could be incited to insurrection

Moments before being machine-gunned to death on September 9, 1939, a weeping boy and two men face their German executioners in the town square of Bydgoszcz, Poland. During the next four months, 10,000 of the city's 140,000 residents were randomly murdered by the Nazis.

by their presumed Jewish overlords. With some exceptions, such as the Polish intelligentsia or Soviet political officers, who were regarded as particularly dangerous, Slavs did not automatically face immediate extinction. Indeed, the Rumanians, Hungarians, and Bulgarians, whose territories were strategically located, or contained vital war industries, actually became wartime allies. Similarly, the Czechs, whose country became a German protectorate in 1939, were generally spared.

The other Slavic peoples were regarded as potential slaves—at least in the short term. The master race was not envisioned as a slave-owning aristocracy, but as a robust rural society that maintained its vigor through its own physical toil. Over a period of time, the Slavs, too, were to be eliminated, their numbers decreasing proportionately to an increasing German presence in the Lebensraum. Genocide would play an inevitable role in this process. As Heinrich Himmler put it, "Our duty in the East is not Germanization in the former sense of the term, that is, imposing German language and laws upon the population, but to ensure that only people of pure German blood inhabit the East."

Few were better qualified to expound on Lebensraum theory than Himmler, who had been captivated from the first by Hitler's atavistic visions of blood and soil. A former chicken farmer and passionate agronomist, the SS chief was particularly taken with the exaggerated reverence for the soil manifest in the theory. That enthusiasm, coupled with his knack for devising ways to transform Hitler's wildest dreams into practical reality, inspired Himmler to create a network of agencies and bureaus devoted to matters of race, ethnicity, and emigration.

One of the largest was the Volksdeutsche Mittelstelle (VOMI), the Liaison Office for Ethnic Germans, founded in 1936 to serve as an intermediary between the Nazi party and the resettled 1.2 million Ethnic Germans who were living in central and eastern Europe. Inside the SS itself was the Race and Settlement Office, which not only monitored the racial purity of SS candidates and their potential brides but also studied rural settlement techniques and devised plans for the eventual establishment of German colonies in the East.

With these and other organizations under SS control, along with the burgeoning SS military arm and the massive state security apparatus that had been crafted by Reinhard Heydrich, Himmler possessed a veritable toolbox of bureaucratic implements for creating the racially pure agricultural utopia he and Hitler envisioned.

The convictions underlying Lebensraum—that living space was essential; that the chosen soil was inhabited by beastlike creatures or deadly bacilli; that only the racially pure deserved the land—perverted the concept of humanity and created among the Nazis an atmosphere in which the destruction of millions of human beings could be contemplated with equanimity. As drummed into the SS, these convictions provided the theoretical fuel for a killing machine, an army of executioners who could set fire to inhabited buildings, shoot pensioners in the back of the head, and kill infants in their mothers' arms with no more remorse or second thoughts than those of butchers or exterminators going about their jobs.

Germany's invasion of Poland offered the world the first concrete evidence that Hitler meant what he said about creating a racially pure society in the East by eliminating its native populations. From the first hours of the war, the invaders went out of their way to kill civilians.

In doing so, they were complying with Hitler's express instructions. As he had made clear to his military commanders on August 22, 1939, "The aim is not the arrival at a certain line but the annihilation of living forces." He authorized them to kill "without pity or mercy all men, women, and children of Polish descent or language. Only in this way can we obtain the living space we need."

No one was safe. From pedestrians on residential streets in Warsaw to shepherds tending their flocks in remote fields, noncombatants were shot, bombed, and strafed with the same ferocity that was unleashed on the overwhelmed Polish army. The carnage was stupefying in both its cruelty and its seeming senselessness. In the Pomeranian city of Bydgoszcz, the "first victims of the campaign were a number of Boy Scouts, from twelve to sixteen years of age, who were set up in the marketplace against a wall and shot," reported a Miss Baker-Beall, an Englishwoman who was living there at the time of the invasion. "No reason was given." Next came a priest, gunned down as he rushed into the square to administer last rites to the murdered boys. In the following few days, thirty-four merchants and tradespeople and the seventeen-year-old son of a local doctor were all herded into the square and machine-gunned.

Scarcely a town or city in western Poland was spared such scenes during the first weeks of the occupation. The American ambassador to Poland, Anthony J. Drexel Biddle, Jr., reported that it seemed to be Germany's intention "to terrorize the civilian population and to reduce the number of childbearing Poles irrespective of category."

In mid-October, Hitler relieved the Wehrmacht of principal responsibility for administering the conquered territories. The subsequent division of Poland into the annexed western provinces and the Government General farther east—which Hitler called the "first colonial territory of the German nation"—set the stage for a full-scale attempt to implement Lebensraum.

A new branch of the SS, the Reich Commission for the Strengthening of Germanism (RKFDV), was set up, incorporating the existing Race and Settlement Office as well as VOMI. The purpose of RKFDV was to plan and carry out the colonization of conquered eastern territories by clearing suitable areas of their Slavic inhabitants and settling Germans in their place. Himmler was given a new title, Reichskommissar for the Strengthening of Germanism. With it went the task of arranging the immediate eviction of 1.5 million Poles from the western provinces to make way for about 500,000 Ethnic Germans to be resettled from the Soviet-controlled Baltic States and eastern Poland, which had been annexed by the Soviet Union in September in accordance with a secret agreement contained in the Hitler-Stalin Pact of August 23.

To determine who would be deported, the RKFDV classified Poles in the western provinces according to their occupational and social status as well as their attitude toward the Germans. Three groups were singled out for immediate removal: Poles who had settled in the area after 1918; Poles who

German colonists arrive in Jelesnia, Poland, beneath a banner reading, "A cordial welcome to your new home." Belying that friendly sentiment, settlers were subjected to harsh restrictions, including racial screening by the SS and ongoing supervision by the police.

A Polish family is evicted from its home to make way for German settlers. Many such families were separated during expulsions—able-bodied members sent to Germany as forced labor, others shipped east.

had worked for the Polish cause; and Poles who belonged to what was broadly defined as the intelligentsia—a category embracing not only teachers, physicians, landowners, writers, and the Catholic clergy but also anyone who had ever attended a secondary school. This last group was a particular target. The annexed portions of Poland were to be purged of their entire political and social elite because the educated classes were thought to be a potential source of leadership for any opposition to Nazi rule.

Moreover, they represented a living reproach to Nazi declarations of the subhuman status of all Poles.

The evictions were swift and brutal. An SS detachment would appear at a house and serve its residents with an evacuation order. Often they were given only twenty minutes to pack a suitcase, and were required to clean the house as well so that things would be tidy for the new occupants. Their luggage could weigh no more than 100 pounds. It could not include valuables; sometimes even wedding rings and gold-rimmed spectacles were confiscated. Everything else—furniture, bedding, books, pots, pans, and the keys to the front door—was left for the incoming German settlers. Any objections were silenced by summary execution.

The deportees were sorted out at transport centers. Young, strong-looking Poles were sent west to Germany as slave laborers. Others were loaded onto trains and taken east to the Government General, where they were often simply deposited at small railroad stations or dumped in open fields and left to their own devices. Many never even made it that far. Jammed into locked, unheated cattle cars in midwinter and often deprived for days of food and water, the deportees died by the hundreds from exposure, malnutrition, and asphyxiation.

Those Poles who were neither deported eastward nor pressed into forced labor in Germany were reduced to the status of nonpersons. Left behind in anticipation of a temporary need for manpower—in part to help the incoming German settlers—they were subjected to a host of brutally oppressive measures designed to turn them into nothing more than expendable slaves. Signs posted on once-Polish establishments read "Entrance Is Forbidden to Poles, Jews, and Dogs." Polish men under the age of twenty-eight and women under twenty-five were not allowed to marry— one of several measures taken to restrict the Polish birthrate. All schools and most churches were shut down. Poles were denied the right to enter any profession. Their children could attend only the first four grades of a German elementary school. Sport was prohibited, because the Nazis felt that physical training conditions a nation for defense—an activity not to be encouraged among slaves.

Life was no better for Poles inside the Government General. Hitler had told Hans Frank that the district was to be regarded as nothing more than one "huge Polish labor camp." Frank was also told that his ultimate job would be to finish off the Poles for good when they were no longer needed as slaves. Frank understood perfectly. "It is our aim that the very concept of Polish be erased for centuries to come," he explained. "Neither the republic, nor any other form of Polish state will ever be reborn."

Accordingly, Frank ordered the wholesale destruction of Polish statues,

Under the eye of a German overseer, Polish women dump newly harvested potatoes into a wagon. Confiscated Polish farmland that was not immediately given to German colonists was reserved for Wehrmacht soldiers' use after the war.

monuments, shrines, theaters, and libraries. Works by Polish artists were either confiscated or destroyed. And although in the privacy of his Krakow castle Frank was known to have entertained his guests by playing the music of Chopin on the piano, the Poles themselves were forbidden to listen to the works of their most celebrated composer. Any expression of Polish patriotism, such as the showing of a Polish flag or the singing of the Polish anthem, was punishable by death.

A Pole could also be shot for failing to doff his hat or yield the sidewalk to an approaching German; children were killed for making anti-German statements. "There never was a moment when we did not feel threatened," recalled Wanda Draczynska, a Warsaw office worker. "Every time we left home, we never knew whether we would ever see it again." Early in 1940, upon hearing that large red posters had been put up in Prague announcing the execution of seven Czechs, Hans Frank boasted, "If I wanted to have a poster put up for every seven Poles who were shot, the forests of Poland would not suffice for producing the paper for such posters."

Sporadic waves of arrests and liquidations killed many hundreds of Poles every month. The sight of people being shot in the street became commonplace. Some Poles, like nineteen-year-old Anna Orska, witnessed even worse: "One day, I saw a woman crossing the road leading a small child by the hand. Suddenly, an SS man went up to her, grabbed the child, and threw it against the wall, killing it instantly. He shouted, 'We have saved a bullet!' I could not forget that sight for many years after."

Poles who were not summarily killed when caught committing a transgression were packed off to one of the concentration camps springing up all over German-occupied Poland. By the end of 1940, at least fifty of the sinister installations webbed the Government General alone. Their original purpose was not assembly-line extermination, but the extraction of slave labor from prisoners at the smallest possible investment in food and upkeep. And yet, long before the first large-scale gassings occurred in late 1941, incarceration in a concentration camp was almost sure to result in death. A Polish Catholic who was in the inaugural transport of 756 prisoners to Auschwitz in June 1940 later calculated that the average life expectancy in the Polish camps was three weeks. People who managed to last much longer were often executed merely on the assumption that they must be stealing food. Ultimately, so many Poles were sent to concentration camps that virtually every Polish family had a member who had died or been tortured in one.

In the first two years of Nazi rule in Poland, Christian Poles were more exposed than Jews to arrest, deportation, and death. During that period, most Jews were herded into ghettos to await the final determination of their fate. By June of 1941, as final plans for the invasion of the Soviet Union were being made, some 30,000 Jews had already perished—about 20,000 from disease and starvation in the Warsaw and Lodz ghettos alone, the remainder in labor camps or as a result of individual shootings, street massacres, and reprisal actions. But Jews had not yet been the target of a deliberate, systematic extermination effort. Operation Barbarossa, as the invasion of Russia was code named, was to mark a critical turning point in German policy toward the Jews.

In planning the invasion, Hitler repeatedly stressed to his commanders that the upcoming war was not merely a conflict between states, but a battle to the finish between two opposing world-views. In this context, the "Jewish-Bolshevik" intelligentsia responsible for Marxism were as much the enemy as was the Red Army. As all Jews were de facto members of this conspiracy, all Jews would have to be exterminated.

Handling that job would be the responsibility of the SS, who would follow the army into the Soviet Union, assuming control of territories and their inhabitants as they fell under the German boot. Also, in a sharp departure from standard German military procedure, a force of SS and other police units was actually to accompany the invading troops. Small, mobile units—special task forces called *Einsatzgruppen*—were charged with ridding the freshly taken territories of their undesirable civilian elements. In order for the plan to be most effective, surprise was essential; thus, the first Ein-

Standing behind his desk at the governor's palace in Krakow, Hans Frank receives fellow members of the Blood Order serving in Poland. The Nazi party's highest decoration, the order was worn by those who had taken part in the 1923 Munich Beer Hall Putsch.

satzgruppen would be required to operate virtually on the front lines.

Less than three months before the invasion, Himmler's able deputy, Security Chief Reinhard Heydrich, met with the Wehrmacht quartermaster general, Eduard Wagner, to hammer out an arrangement whereby the army and the SS could carry out their tasks simultaneously without getting in each other's way. By March 26, the pair had produced a draft plan outlining a unique partnership between the two groups. Functionally—that is, in pursuit of their so-called special duties—the Einsatzgruppen were to take their orders from the SS. Otherwise, they were subject to military command. The army was to control their movements and furnish them with quarters, rations, gasoline, and communications assistance.

There were to be four groups, designated A through D, each attached to one of the four army groups that would penetrate the Soviet Union along a 1,350-mile front. Each Einsatzgruppe was approximately battalion size.

Their total strength was not large: some 3,000 men (and a handful of women). Because of the special character of their work, however, there was a higher ratio of officers to soldiers than in a unit of comparable size.

By and large, Einsatzgruppen troops came from the Waffen-SS, the Order Police, and the Criminal Police. Some were picked because they had already demonstrated exceptional callousness and brutality in the performance of other duties; many of the Waffen-SS were assigned as a form of punishment and discipline for a poor performance. The officers, on the other hand, were chosen according to different standards. Heydrich wanted leaders who could bring intelligence, discipline, and resourcefulness to their tasks, and he found them among the ranks of Germany's best-educated young professionals. Many were lawyers in their civilian lives; their number also included a physician and a professional opera singer. Most were ambitious men in their thirties who had already enjoyed considerable professional success. Nothing in their backgrounds suggested sociopathic or criminal tendencies. Otto Ohlendorf, commander of Einsatzgruppe D, was typical. Widely regarded as an intellectual, he was a tall, handsome thirty-four-year-old lawyer who held advanced degrees in economics and jurisprudence. Years later, he would try to justify his actions on ethical grounds by citing historical precedents, such as the killing of Gypsies in the Thirty Years War.

As the date of the invasion, June 22, drew near, Ohlendorf and the other young Einsatzgruppen commanders were given pep talks that bolstered the rationale for the acts they were expected to perform. During one briefing, Himmler addressed the officers personally, stressing the importance of their work in eliminating Jews and Communist functionaries. In the meantime, the Reich Central Security Office personnel chief, Bruno Streckenbach, spoke to the rank and file, exhorting them to proceed ruthlessly. For all that, discussions of the exact nature of the Einsatzgruppen's duties evidently remained so couched in euphemism that even at fairly high levels within the SS there was still room for uncertainty regarding just what the special squads were expected to do. Finally, at a meeting of about fifty SS leaders in Berlin, a member of the Gestapo asked Heydrich point-blank: "We should shoot the Jews?"

Heydrich replied coolly, "Of course."

When Operation Barbarossa began, five million Jews lived in the Soviet Union. Most were concentrated in the western sections overrun by the German blitzkrieg that summer. With every day of the advance, thousands more Jews found themselves trapped behind the German lines.

To find and liquidate them, the Einsatzgruppen were divided into de-

tachments called *Einsatzkommandos*, approximately the size of a military company. These units, usually with the aid of regular army troops, would enter a town and start rounding up civilian targets—Jews and Communist leaders—working from information supplied by local collaborators and lists prepared ahead of time by military intelligence.

Once the victims had been assembled, they were marched off to be executed out of sight of the local populace. Small Jewish communities of a few hundred to a few thousand could be slaughtered in a single day. In larger towns and cities, such as Vilna, Lithuania, where the Jewish population numbered 57,000, the Jews were herded roughly into makeshift ghettos, from which they were later taken in groups to execution sites. Those who somehow escaped the first wave of fast-moving killer squads were often eliminated by mop-up crews of SS that came in to administer the captured territories.

In many areas, the Germans were assisted in their ugly work by local anti-Semites, who not only helped round up Jews, but enthusiastically joined in the killings. As a unit of Einsatzgruppe A arrived in Kaunas, Lithuania, local partisans were fighting Red Army troops who had occupied their country only a year earlier. When the Soviets retreated, the German commander persuaded the Lithuanian chief to help gather up the Jews. The partisans responded with such fervor that within a few days they had killed some 5,000 Jews. In many parts of the Baltic States and in the Ukraine, local police and militiamen by the score joined the Einsatzgruppen as murder gangs.

The speed of the advance and the element of surprise rendered the Jews all but defenseless. Bewildered, unarmed, and surrounded, they could not mount an effective resistance. Furthermore, at least in the first weeks of the campaign, the Jews were not only stunned by the ferocity of the attacks on them, but also shocked that the Germans, of all people, should be doing such things. Historically, the Jews of Russia had regarded Germany as a bastion of culture and enlightenment compared to the medieval religious hatreds of their own land. Consequently, many unsuspecting Jews— particularly older ones who warmly remembered the courtesy and civility of the Germans who had occupied their country in World War I—actually looked forward to the arrival of the Germans.

"The Jews are remarkably ill informed about our attitude toward them," reported a German intelligence officer in July. "They do not know how the Jews are treated in Germany, or for that matter, in Warsaw. They believe that we shall leave them in peace if they mind their own business and work diligently." The Einsatzgruppen were quick to exploit this attitude, in many cases using it to dupe Jews up to the last minute. Occasionally, they would

An SS man shouts orders at a group of Jews gathered for deportation from Grodno in the Soviet Union. Jews who escaped the killer squads that followed the German army into Russia in 1941 were held in ghettos to await later extermination.

enter a town or village, contact the local rabbi, and ask politely for Jewish volunteers for some type of work. Then they would march the group off to be murdered and come back for more.

In most cases, the Jews were assembled at a collection point and taken to the killing site a small batch at a time; the soldiers were taught to be reassuring so their victims would not panic. At the site, a grave was prepared. Sometimes a bomb crater or antitank ditch could be found; frequently, the Jews were handed shovels and told to start digging. When the grave was ready, the victims were ordered to surrender their money, watches, and other valuables. Then often, just before they were lined up on the edge of the ditch to be shot, they were ordered to strip—both to salvage their clothing and to further break their will to fight.

Some futilely resisted nonetheless. "Our father did not want to undress," said Rivka Yosselevscka, who miraculously survived a massacre at Zagrodski, near Pinsk. "He did not want to stand naked. They tore the clothing off the old man, and he was shot." In the next few minutes, Rivka stood frozen, holding her daughter in her arms, and watched her entire family die. First her mother was shot, then her eighty-year-old grandmother and the two children she was holding. Next her aunt, also with children in her arms, was killed. Then came Rivka's two sisters, and finally it was her turn. "I felt the German take the child from my arms. The child cried out and was shot immediately. Then he aimed at me. He aimed the revolver at me and ordered me to watch, then turned my head around and shot me. Then I fell into the pit amongst the bodies." Rivka, wounded in the head, played dead and crawled away after the soldiers left.

Some commanders disapproved of the single-bullet method. Otto Ohlendorf insisted on mass fire from a distance to protect his men against possible future charges of personal responsibility for any individual death. Ohlendorf was similarly concerned about the psychological effect of the work on his troops, and he visited killing operations often to ensure that they were carried out in a correct military manner. Otherwise, explained his adjutant, Heinz Schubert, "The psychic burden would have been too much for the execution commando."

Not all the murders were accomplished with such German efficiency and dispatch, particularly in areas where local police or militiamen were given their heads and allowed to deal with Jews in their own way. On July 28, SS Sergeant Felix Landau described in his diary the scene that greeted him earlier that day when he drove into Drogobych to the local prison, and found the town turned into an abattoir. "The streets tell of murder," he wrote. "Hundreds of Jews with bloodstained faces, with bullet holes in the head, broken limbs, gouged-out eyes, run ahead of us. One of the Jews carries another one, who is bleeding to death. We drive to the prison. Here we see things no one has ever seen before. It is absolutely impossible to describe them. Two soldiers stand at the entrance to the prison. Wielding sticks as big as fists, they lash furiously at the crowd. Jews are being pushed out from inside. Covered with blood, they collapse on top of one another— they scream like pigs. We stand and look on."

In Berlin, far away from such scenes, Heydrich received only the dry field reports from his Einsatzgruppen officers: RSHA IV-A-1, Operational Report USSR no. 94 from September 25, 1941, reported 75,000 liquidations in Lithuania in response to a rise in Jewish propaganda; RSHA IV-A-1, Operational Report USSR no. 58 from August 20, 1941, detailed the extermination of 4,500 Jews in Pinsk in retaliation for the death of a local militiaman. As sterile and bureaucratic as these reports were, however, together they did reveal that within the first five weeks of the German invasion of Russia, the number of Jews killed in the newly captured territory exceeded the total number killed in all the previous years of the Nazi regime. On August 1, Heydrich wrote to Himmler, "It may be safely assumed that in the future there will be no more Jews in the annexed eastern territories."

Not long afterward, Himmler decided to see for himself how things were going. Accompanied by General Karl Wolff, chief of his personal staff, he visited the SS operations center at Minsk, where a small demonstration was arranged for his benefit. One hundred prisoners were taken out to an open grave, ordered to jump in a few at a time, and told to lie face down. Each group in turn was then shot from above. Himmler, who, according to Wolff, "had never seen dead people before," stepped up to get a better look at the killing. "While he was looking in," Wolff recalled, "Himmler got a splash of brains on his coat. I think they also splashed into his face. He went very green and pale. He wasn't actually sick, but he was heaving, and he turned around and swayed." Wolff jumped forward to steady the shaky Reichsführer-SS and led him away.

After he had recovered his composure, Himmler gathered the shooting

A bloodbath commences on the streets of Kaunas, Lithuania, on June 28, 1941, four days after the Germans occupied the city. Egged on by the invaders, Lithuanian police and a group of released convicts beat hundreds of Jews to death with iron bars.

squad around him and gave a speech. The men had undoubtedly noticed, he said, how deeply affected he had been by what he had just seen. He had been aroused to the depths of his soul. It was a hateful business, he continued, and he would not like it if Germans did such things gladly. But he assured the men that they were doing their duty in accordance with a higher law. He encouraged them to look at nature, where constant combat was the rule. The weak must go under, he explained. Mankind must decide what is harmful and defend itself. Vermin must be destroyed.

Later, Himmler spoke privately to his commanders about devising a less traumatic method of killing than shooting. The immediate result of his request was an experiment in which dynamite was used to blow up mental patients. Evidently the results were deemed unacceptable, and RSHA's technical branch came up with a far more successful method—the gas van. Large trucks were modified so that their poisonous carbon-monoxide exhaust fumes would be conducted to their sealed interiors. Each Ein-

In October 1942, Jewish women and children from the Ukrainian village of Misocz are herded naked to their communal grave (above). A Ukrainian policeman, enlisted to aid in the killings, aims his weapon at still-moving victims who survived the initial rounds of gunfire (right). In that same month, more than 80,000 people were murdered in similar pits throughout the German-occupied Soviet Union.

satzgruppe received two of the mobile killing devices in 1941; others were dispatched to Poland. Yet despite their effectiveness, the gas vans had a major drawback. They were too small. Their average capacity was less than fifty people—inadequate both for the scale of mass murders being committed daily in the East and for the even more massive killings Berlin was contemplating for the future.

For the time being, the most practical method of extermination remained marching victims away a handful at a time and tumbling them with bullets into blood-drenched ditches and ravines. When it was well organized, that could be an extremely effective method indeed, as was soon to be demonstrated outside Kiev in a deep natural cleft in the earth known as Old Woman's Gully—Babi Yar.

In mid-September, the German army captured Kiev, the Soviet Union's third-largest city. The victors lost no time in handling the city's Jewish

inhabitants. The panzer divisions that had taken the city pulled out and headed toward their next objective, Moscow. The SS, in collaboration with Ukrainian police, took over the city's government. Less than two weeks later, on September 28, a curt notice, its text printed in Russian, Ukrainian, and German, appeared on buildings, tree trunks, and fence posts. It ordered all Jews in Kiev and its suburbs to report the following day to the old Jewish cemetery on the outskirts of town not far from a railroad station. The notice suggested that the Jews were going to be resettled.

The next morning the Jews came out, many leaving their homes before dawn so they could board the trains early in order to find seats. By 7:00 a.m., the streets leading to the cemetery were packed with people loaded down with bundles or pushing wheelbarrows, handcarts, or baby carriages.

The crowd moved so slowly that it was afternoon before those who had started at daybreak reached the cemetery. As they approached, they could hear the sound of machine-gun fire. People in the crowd speculated uneasily about the shots, but few could believe that the Germans were actually machine-gunning innocent civilians en masse. Even as they passed through the cemetery gate and were instructed to set down their packages—clothing and knapsacks on the left, food on the right—people reassured one another that their belongings would be sent on by baggage car and sorted out when they reached their destination. But there were no trains. The now empty-handed Jews were divided into groups of ten and sent on, one batch at a time.

As the little groups drew closer to their still unknown destination, the soldiers along the path became more numerous until they stood shoulder to shoulder, creating a corridor about five feet wide. These men had their sleeves rolled up, they held thick rubber truncheons or big sticks, and they were yelling, *"Schnell, Schnell!"*—hurry, hurry! Vicious blows rained down on the people, whose cries and screams blended with the jeers and shouts of the soldiers and the barking of dogs, creating a terrible din.

Some Jews fell and were trampled where they lay. The rest staggered into a clearing filled with Ukrainian police, who seized them and shouted at them to undress. Those who hesitated were kicked, beaten with clubs and brass knuckles, and forcibly stripped. Then little groups were led naked through a narrow gap in an earthen bank to an area from which came the steady bursts of gunfire.

The operation went quickly except when women clung tightly to their children or fumbled as they tried to help the smaller ones undress. Now and then, a German or Ukrainian would impatiently snatch a child from its mother and hurl it over the bank.

Watching this awful sight from a small rise was a group of about fifty

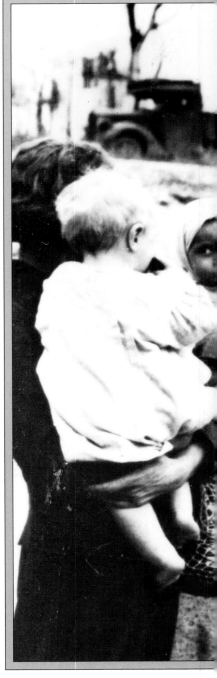

Touring the eastern front in August 1941, SS chief Heinrich Himmler visits a destroyed Soviet village and meets its inhabitants, a group that could expect little sympathy from him. Himmler later said of the "subhuman" Slavs, "It is a crime against our own blood to worry about them."

people who had managed to persuade the guards that they were not Jewish, but had been caught in the crowd by accident. As it grew dark and the operation seemed to be winding down for the day, an open car drew into the clearing carrying a tall, elegantly dressed German officer. He looked over at the group huddled on the little hill. "Shoot them," he snapped. "If even one of them gets away, we won't get a single Jew tomorrow." The guards scurried to obey, hastily herding the group through the gap in the earth without taking the time to make them remove their clothes.

They emerged from the passage onto the brow of a deep ravine. A narrow ledge had been freshly cut into one sheer sandy wall of the canyon. Directly opposite, across the cleft, was a line of machine guns. The group was motioned out onto the ledge. Far below, the floor of the ravine was carpeted with bloody, naked bodies.

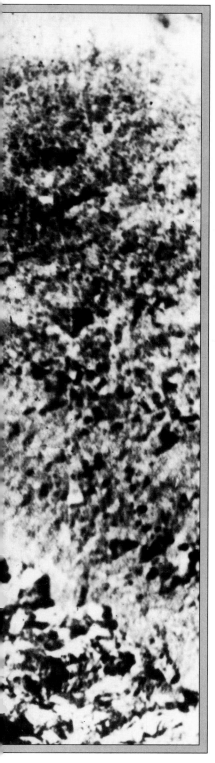

Germans gaze down on the dead at Babi Yar, where some 200,000 Russians were killed by the Nazis during two years of occupation. In August 1943, the decomposing bodies were excavated and burned in a furnace that was built of granite tombstones taken from the city's Jewish cemetery.

Just as the order to fire was barked out, Dina Mironovna Pronicheva, an actress from the Kiev Puppet Theater and the mother of two small children back in town, made a desperate effort to save her life. An instant before the bullets hit, she hurled herself into space, diving straight into the mass of corpses. As she landed, she recalled later, it felt as if she had fallen into a warm sea of blood. The thick, sticky liquid splashed over her as she lay perfectly still, with her eyes closed, her arms outstretched. Beneath and all around her she felt steady undulating motion. Many of the victims were still alive, and the whole mass gently stirred, settling down deeper and tighter with the movements.

Soldiers shone flashlights into the gloom of the pit, aiming their pistols at any signs of life. Some of them jumped down and waded through corpses, shooting at anything that moved. An SS man stumbled over Dina, yanked her limp form up for a closer look, then dropped her back down, giving her a sharp kick and stepping hard on her hand as he turned away.

Then the Germans clambered out of the gully; minutes later, there was a command to "Shovel away" and the sound of sand thudding on bodies. Still lying limp, Pronicheva did not stir as the fill rose around her. Finally, when the sand started to get in her mouth, she clawed herself free and slowly made her way to the gully wall, then climbed silently out under cover of darkness. She was joined by one other survivor, a boy who had also managed to crawl out (only to be found and shot some hours later). Dina Pronicheva lived to tell the awful tale. On that day and the following one, 33,771 people died at Babi Yar.

The Germans made a concerted effort to keep such massacres secret, never publishing information about them and forbidding soldiers and others who had taken part to talk about them. As late as February 1942, Reinhard Heydrich assured a group of regional commanders that the extermination of the Jews was proceeding so smoothly that local populations hardly noticed what was going on.

By then, however, no one in the occupied East could have failed to notice what was happening. Villagers who had seen the Jews marched off and then heard shots ringing out from nearby woods and fields realized the truth. In the many areas where the SS had recruited the local people to help them, the native police and militiamen told their relatives and neighbors. Sometimes, massacres had one or two miraculous survivors like Rivka Yosselevscka or Dina Pronicheva.

And despite the official policy of secrecy, the slaughter of the Jews was a sensation among the troops. Although the killing sites were off-limits to ordinary soldiers unless they were detailed to help out, hundreds of them slipped away to witness the executions. Not only did they watch, they took pictures, wrote letters, and talked. Inevitably, the news spread throughout the occupied territories and began to filter back to Germany.

The army attempted in vain to stem the flow of information. Once people knew about it, they could not keep it to themselves. There had been pogroms before, Jewish villages raided and sacked. And the Soviet people under Stalin were grimly familiar with death on a massive scale. But no one had ever seen or heard of anything quite like the methodical, systematic extermination now taking place in their midst. And while Soviets on the whole voiced few objections to the principle of killing Jews, the dramatic reality of it left many of them aghast.

A German stationed in Borizov, in Belorussia, spoke to a number of Russians shortly before the massacre of all the Jews who lived there. "Let them perish; they did us a lot of harm," said his landlord breezily, expressing a common sentiment. But on the following morning, after the Jews had been marched off, the whole town seemed to be in shock. "Who ordered such a thing?" they whispered. "What have these poor Jews done? How is it possible to kill 6,500 Jews all at once?"

During the following months, the Germans in Borizov saw the natives' initial feelings of horror and disbelief give way to a wave of mysticism, premonitions, dream interpretations, and superstitions. People searched their Bibles for prophecies to explain what was happening to the Jews— and for clues to their own fates. "When will it be our turn?" they asked themselves. All through the occupied territories people were asking that same question. In Kiev, they answered it with a blackly facetious ditty: "Jews kaput, Gypsies too; and then the Ukrainians, then comes you."

The savage German reply was not long in coming. The occupied territories were divided into two spheres of responsibility: the Theater of Military Operations (where the fighting was still going on) and the Military Administrative Zone. The latter acquired a civilian administration that answered to a new agency, the Reich Ministry for Eastern Occupied Territories, headed by Nazi party philosopher Alfred Rosenberg. The zone consisted of two sections: "Ostland," which covered the Baltic States and Belorussia, and "Ukraine," made up of the bulk of the Ukraine proper and the parts of eastern Poland that had earlier been occupied by the Soviets. (The Government General of Poland was now slated to be annexed directly to the Reich for settlement by Germans.)

The fate of the natives of these areas depended in large part on the Nazis' conception of where they fell on the racial scale. The Estonians were believed to be racially German; Latvians and Lithuanians were considered partially German. On the whole, this meant that their lives would be spared.

Elsewhere in the Soviet Union, the natives were regarded unequivocally as subhuman and thus were subject to deportation to Asiatic Russia, slavery, or extermination, in keeping with the blueprint for Lebensraum.

The 40 million Ukrainians—whose hatred for Soviet and Russian oppression was so intense that they had welcomed German soldiers with flowers and balalaika music—soon became the target of brutal measures. Their fertile land—the Soviet Union's breadbasket and a major industrial center—was the most coveted territory in the Lebensraum scheme. Hitler called it "this big cake," and he had no intention of sharing it with those he regarded as "helots, subhumans, and monkeys."

Hitler's choice for administrator of the Ukraine, Erich Koch, seemed the perfect man for the job. "I am known as a brutal dog," Koch told his subordinates in September 1941. "That is why I was chosen Reichskommissar. Our task is to suck from the Ukraine all the goods we can get hold of without consideration of the feelings or the property of the Ukrainians. I am expecting from you the utmost severity toward the native population."

Koch's approach to exploiting and depopulating the Ukraine was to employ a methodical program that would quickly rid the region of Jews and Gypsies, then decimate the remaining population through artificially induced famine, massive deportations, and massacres triggered by the slightest provocations.

The conditions for famine were cold-bloodedly set in motion at a conference in November 1941, when it was decided to intercept food deliveries to all large Ukrainian cities as well as to regions already suffering wartime food shortages. The supplies were to be diverted to the Reich and the German army at the expense of what the official report of the meeting called "superfluous eaters (Jews and the population of Ukrainian cities)."

By then, the Ukraine was in the grip of the kind of institutionalized terrorism that had engulfed Poland earlier. As in Poland, no one could be sure he or she would be spared sudden, arbitrary death. Gypsies were subject to the same immediate extermination as Jews, and dark-haired, dark-complected people lived in terror of their lives. Recalled one Ukrainian, "The fascists hunted Gypsies as if they were game."

On October 22, a notice was posted in Kiev, informing the citizenry that 100 residents had been shot in retaliation for an act of sabotage. On November 2, Major General Friedrich Eberhardt, military commandant of the city, citing the persistent danger of arson and sabotage, issued an order declaring that 300 hostages would be shot for the next such incident. By the end of the month, the number had been raised to 400.

These orders came amid a flood of directives covering a bewildering variety of infractions, from refusing to turn in felt boots to failing to inform

Accused of having shot Germans, two Belorussians are hanged in Minsk in 1941. Alleged partisan activity was often used as an

excuse to randomly execute civilians. "It gives us a chance to exterminate whoever opposes us," commented Hitler.

on Jews. Disobedience of the most trivial rule could mean summary execution. Curfew violators were shot on the spot and their bodies left on the sidewalks. On October 26, a number of pigeon fanciers were sent to their deaths at Babi Yar—where executions continued to be conducted—because they had failed to read the papers that morning and thus had missed an order demanding they destroy their flocks.

After word of this misfortune spread, the first topic of daily conversation was: "What is the latest order?" But even the most scrupulously law-abiding Ukrainians might still be seized in the aftermath of an anti-German act—dragged from their homes at night or rounded up in a suddenly cordoned-off section of the city—until the SS had gathered up the required number of reprisal victims.

In the Ukraine and elsewhere in the occupied territories, able-bodied men and women were shipped off to Germany for forced labor. By the summer of 1942, more than one million Soviet civilians had been enslaved. Other slave laborers came from the ranks of the 5.7 million Soviet prisoners of war, the largest single group of Nazi victims other than the Jews.

In May 1942, while the killings in the East continued unabated, Himmler's SS planners in Berlin drew up a blueprint for repopulating with Germans the lands that were being stripped of their native inhabitants. According to the General Plan East, European Russia would be colonized by Germans who arrived in a series of frontier marches. During the long settlement phase, which was estimated to span several generations, military strongpoints would protect the German enclaves against any hostile natives. To ensure a tough breed of pioneer, war veterans would be given priority as colonists.

A few of the Slavs would be allowed to remain in the colonized areas as a source of cheap labor. None of them, however, would be permitted to own land or capital. The rest of the Slavic population was to be driven east of the Urals into Siberia and central Asia. Himmler recognized that these forced exiles would pose a threat to his pioneers, but he saw that as a plus. "The perpetual eastern military frontier," he blithely predicted, "will always keep us young."

That grotesque empire in the East never materialized. Potential German colonists were understandably reluctant to flock eastward into the midst of a titanic struggle between two massive armies; General Plan East was temporarily shelved. The closest it came to fruition was the establishment of a few German enclaves along the Krakow-Kiev and Odessa-Leningrad routes in order to protect communications lines vital to the war effort.

Nonetheless, the fantastic, obsessive planning and brutal killing went on right up to the end of the war. When it was all over, an estimated 13 million

In the bitter winter of 1941-1942, Soviet prisoners of war in an internment camp stack the stripped corpses of fellow inmates on a wagon. Of the Soviet soldiers who surrendered to German forces during the war, more than three million either died in captivity of exposure, disease, and starvation, or were killed outright by the SS.

eastern Europeans had been sacrificed on the bloody altar of Nazi racism. In the Ukraine alone, as many as 4 million noncombatants, including approximately 900,000 Jews, were killed. More than half of Kiev's prewar population of 900,000 perished; between 150,000 and 200,000 were slaughtered at Babi Yar. Countless others starved to death or were deported to Germany, many never to return. In Belorussia, an estimated 2.3 million civilians—1 out of every 4 in the population—were killed; 200 towns and 9,200 villages were destroyed.

In Poland, the final toll was 6 million dead—22 percent of the total population. About half the victims were Christians, the other half Jews. The killing storm devoured more than half of Poland's educated classes, including 45 percent of its physicians, 57 percent of its attorneys, and 40 percent of its professors. More than 2,600 priests were killed; Polish journalists were rendered all but extinct.

After the Germans had been driven out of Kiev, fourteen-year-old Anatoly Kuznetsov, who lived in a small town outside the city, went with a friend to Babi Yar, where they, like many other youngsters, had played as children. For two years, the place had been surrounded by electrified barbed-wire fencing. It had echoed day after day with machine-gun fire. For three weeks in 1943, thick black smoke had blanketed the ravine; according to rumor, that was when the Germans had dug up all the bodies, stacked them like cordwood, and burned them to remove the evidence of a mass grave.

The two boys made their way to the bottom of the ravine to a stream where they had once splashed and skipped stones, but they noticed a change. Then, the streambed had been a uniform grainy sand. Now, it was covered with white pebbles.

Anatoly bent down and picked up one of the pebbles. It was not a pebble after all, but a burned piece of bone, the size of a fingernail, white on top, black on the bottom. The boys followed the stream to its source, a sandy area where the water bubbled up from the ground, washing the bones up with it. They continued walking until they reached a place where the sand was gray and fine. "Suddenly, we realized we were walking on human ashes," Kuznetsov recalled. Nearby, a sandbank had caved in, exposing a granite outcropping and a ten-inch-thick stratum that looked like a vein of coal. Three little boys—goatherds about eight years of age—were chipping away at the coal-like substance and crushing the lumps on the granite while their flock grazed nearby. One of the boys reached into his pocket and fished out a half-melted gold ring that he had found. "I picked up one lump that weighed about five pounds, carried it off, and kept it," Kuznetsov said. "It was the ashes of many people, all mixed together."

As young Anatoly well knew, it was only through luck that his own ashes were not among them. Some years later, he sat down and made a list of all the times he could have been killed according to the various occupation rules. He counted twenty capital offenses, including failing to betray a Jew (he had not turned in his pal Shurka, a half-Jewish boy who had been his playmate since infancy), violating curfew, harboring anti-German sentiments, and owning a pair of felt boots. In addition, he and his mother had hidden in their own home for forty days after having been ordered to evacuate the area. For this, Anatoly added forty more times he might have been shot before he turned fourteen.

"And all this without being a member of the Communist party, the Young Communist League, or the underground. Nor was I a Jew, a Gypsy, or a hostage. I had not made any speeches or owned pigeons or a radio. I was just a most ordinary, average, nondescript little fellow in a cap. But by their rule, I did not have the right to live." ✚

A stern-visaged Reinhard Heydrich returns a salute in the courtyard of Prague's ninth-century Hradcany Castle. At his right is SS Lieut. General Karl-Hermann Frank, who laid the groundwork for Heydrich's plan to Germanize Czechoslovakia.

Demise of a Consummate Nazi

Reinhard Heydrich jockeyed hard for his appointment as Reich protector for Bohemia and Moravia, pushing aside an ailing incumbent and bypassing his SS boss, the suspicious Heinrich Himmler, to win a post that would tie his fate to that of millions in occupied Czechoslovakia. Arriving in Prague in the early fall of 1941, he established his headquarters at Hradcany Castle, home to Bohemian royalty and the famous jeweled crown that was named after the duke of Wenceslas.

"My task," Heydrich declared, "is to teach the Czech people that they cannot deny the reality of their relationship with the Reich, nor avoid the obedience that the Reich demands." Within twenty-four hours, he was signing death warrants; within two months, he had arrested 4,000 people and executed 400 of them.

As a career step, the protectorate presented the designer of Hitler's concentration-camp system with an opportunity to nazify a vast new territory. Heydrich blatantly consolidated his authority by retaining leadership of the powerful Reich Central Security Office and the Einsatzgruppen in the East: He would shuttle between Prague and Berlin to continue his role in preparing for the final solution.

Heydrich drew up plans for the tapping of Czech resources to bolster the German offensive against Russia. "I need calm in the region so that the Czech worker will perform to the best of his ability for the German war machine," he announced during a speech made early in his regime.

He enforced economic discipline with a "whip and sugar" policy. Whereas he simply had political offenders shot, he saw to it that economic criminals—hoarders and black marketeers—were publicly hanged. Among the 400 initial victims of his death sentences were a far greater number of racketeers than former Czech military officers and twice as many butchers as intellectuals. Simultaneously, he encouraged productivity by raising pensions, increasing rations for industrial workers, and opening luxury hotels to common laborers. Ironically, it was worry over the success of Heydrich's program that prompted Czechs living in England to organize a risky operation to kill him.

A Fatal Sense of Security

"Why should my Czechs shoot at me?" snapped Heydrich, spurning the armed security insisted on by other Nazis. However, the regularity of the protector of Prague's daily commute from his villa fifteen miles north of the city did not go unobserved by British-trained agents Josef Gabcik and Jan Kubis, who had parachuted into their homeland in December of 1941.

After months of scouting, the agents planned an assassination on the morning of May 27, 1942. After posting a lookout to signal the approach of Heydrich's Mercedes-Benz, they waited at a streetcar stop, Gabcik with a raincoat draped over a submachine gun, Kubis with grenades in a briefcase.

At 10:30 a.m., Heydrich rode by. He glimpsed Gabcik pointing a Sten gun at him—a weapon that jammed and clicked impotently. But Kubis's grenade exploded under the right rear wheel of the car. Amid the screams of onlookers, Heydrich staggered out of the vehicle, drew his pistol, and fired at the fleeing agents. But within minutes, he collapsed. His driver, an SS sergeant named Klein, gave futile chase as the Czechs escaped, Gabcik on foot, Kubis by bicycle.

In one of his final official appearances, Heydrich (center) arrives to inspect a hospital train that is to be presented as a birthday present to Hitler. His driver sits behind the wheel.

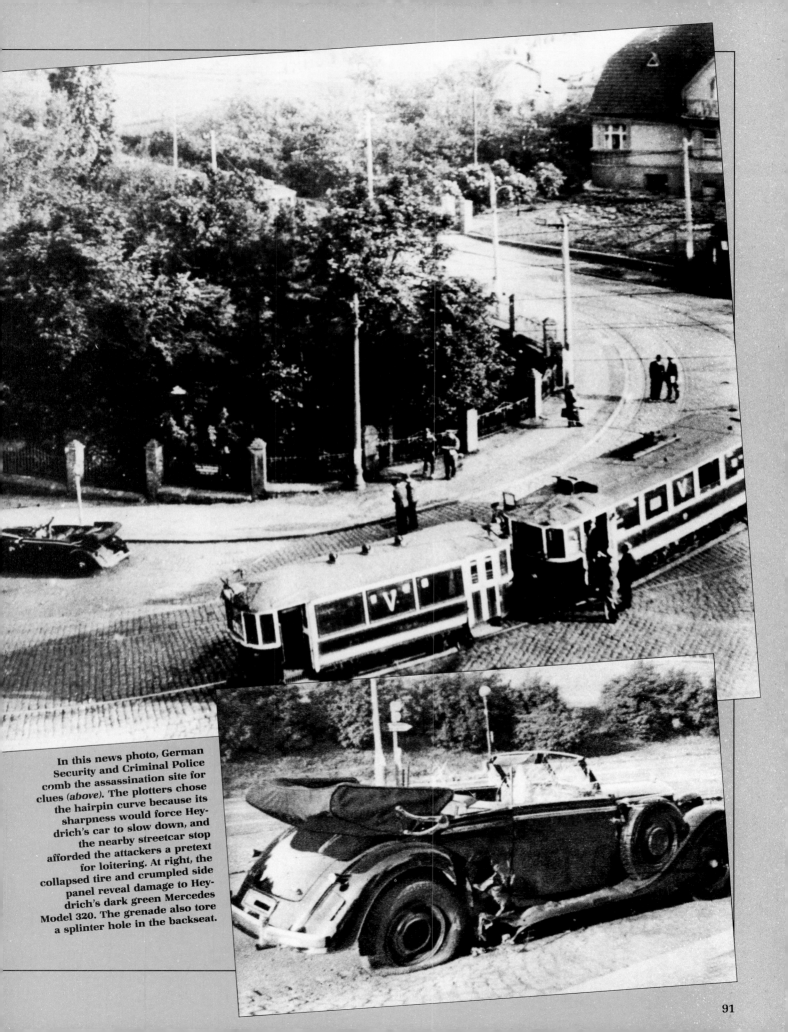

In this news photo, German Security and Criminal Police comb the assassination site for clues (*above*). The plotters chose the hairpin curve because its sharpness would force Heydrich's car to slow down, and the nearby streetcar stop afforded the attackers a pretext for loitering. At right, the collapsed tire and crumpled side panel reveal damage to Heydrich's dark green Mercedes Model 320. The grenade also tore a splinter hole in the backseat.

Heydrich's flag-draped casket leaves the courtyard of Hradcany Castle on a gun carriage, attended by Nazi officials and Wehrmacht troops. Beneath the ornate wrought-iron archway, SS chief Himmler stands flanked by Heydrich's two young sons.

Eulogy for "A Man with a Heart of Iron"

"After what Heydrich has done for these Czechs!" Hitler exclaimed angrily on learning of the attack on his representative. The Führer declared a state of siege in the protectorate, offered a reward of one million marks for the capture of the assassins, and vowed to slaughter 10,000 Czechs. Within days, 13,119 people were arrested, 232 were executed for expressing approval of the attack, and 462 more were executed for possessing weapons or disobeying the police.

In Prague's Bulovka Hospital, Heydrich lay for a week with a broken rib, a pierced diaphragm, and a grenade splinter jutting into his spleen. He insisted on being treated by a German doctor. The prognosis for his recovery remained optimistic; then suddenly, on June 4, the protector died of blood poisoning.

At an elaborate state funeral held in Berlin, Himmler concealed his rivalry with his former protégé. During the day's longest speech, he called Heydrich an "ideal always to be emulated, but perhaps never again to be achieved."

In the Reich Chancellery, Hitler posthumously awards Heydrich the German Order, the Reich's most distinguished medal. After the ceremony ended, he whispered to aides that Heydrich was "a man with a heart of iron."

"We Shall Never Surrender"

Three weeks after the ambush of Heydrich, SS investigators were stumped. The assassins, after moving between prearranged safe houses, were secreted with several confederates in the crypt of an Orthodox church. But then the SS men got their break.

Karel Curda, a Czech parachutist who had trained in Britain with the assassins, switched loyalties and betrayed the agents' hideout.

At dawn on June 18, two lines of SS troops opened fire on the church, mortally wounding three of the agents. The SS demanded surrender. "We are Czechs; we shall never surrender!" replied the four surviving men. The SS tried tossing tear-gas canisters and pumping water and smoke into the crypt. Finally, they dynamited open a huge slab covering a second entrance to the crypt. The two-hour siege ended when the Germans entered to find four wet and bloody bodies: The killers of Heydrich had used their last bullets on themselves.

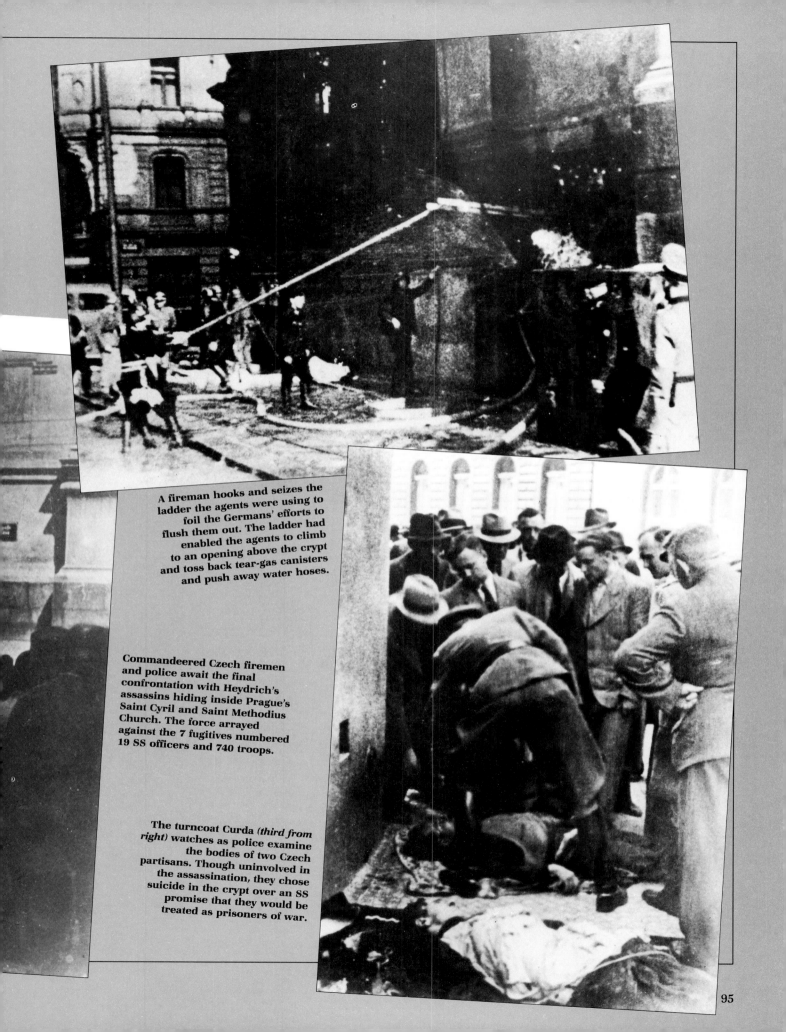

A fireman hooks and seizes the ladder the agents were using to foil the Germans' efforts to flush them out. The ladder had enabled the agents to climb to an opening above the crypt and toss back tear-gas canisters and push away water hoses.

Commandeered Czech firemen and police await the final confrontation with Heydrich's assassins hiding inside Prague's Saint Cyril and Saint Methodius Church. The force arrayed against the 7 fugitives numbered 19 SS officers and 740 troops.

The turncoat Curda *(third from right)* watches as police examine the bodies of two Czech partisans. Though uninvolved in the assassination, they chose suicide in the crypt over an SS promise that they would be treated as prisoners of war.

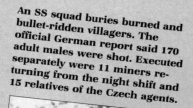

An SS squad buries burned and bullet-ridden villagers. The official German report said 170 adult males were shot. Executed separately were 11 miners returning from the night shift and 15 relatives of the Czech agents.

SS men patrol the ruins of Lidice. The Germans reported removing 84,000 square yards of rubble from the razed village, which they then plowed over and planted with grain to remove any trace of habitation.

The Obliteration of Lidice

Hours after Heydrich's funeral, SS Security Police surrounded Lidice, a village near Prague, and herded the population into the square. The villagers were suspected of harboring Heydrich's assassins, and now the SS sought revenge. Grinning as they worked, the SS culled the women and children for shipment to concentration camps, then lined up the men in groups of ten and shot them. Impatient with the pace of the killing, the commander forced the remaining men into a barn and set it ablaze. The Germans then torched the rest of the village.

The Institutions of Genocide

ate in the spring of 1942, Reinhard Heydrich lay dying, the victim of an armed attack by members of the Czech Resistance in Prague. Even as he passed his last hours, his colleagues in the SS were shaping his final legacy. Code-named Operation Reinhard in his honor, this new phase in the final solution was the logical follow-up to the massive round of killings carried out by the Einsatzgruppen. But Operation Reinhard was even more ambitious: It called for nothing less than the systematic extermination through gas poisoning of the estimated two million Jews concentrated in the ghettos of the Government General and in the incorporated territories of Poland. The operation already was under way at two new Polish camps, Belzec and Sobibor, and would soon be launched at a third, which was nearing completion at Treblinka.

These three camps stood out uniquely among the hundreds of such installations built by the Germans in Poland. Most of the camps housed groups of forced laborers; some were compounds for prisoners of war; others were concentration camps of the type pioneered in the Reich at Dachau and Buchenwald, where Jews and others were detained, tortured, worked to death, or executed. At all of these camps, and in the ghettos of Poland, the killing would continue through 1942 and beyond; inmates would die from hunger, disease, and maltreatment as well as from actual executions. Gas chambers were installed at two large concentration camps: Majdanek in eastern Poland and Auschwitz in Upper Silesia, one of the provinces of western Poland that had been annexed by the Reich. Auschwitz, in fact, would exterminate so many Jews that it became practically synonymous with the Holocaust. But both of these places maintained labor camps and thus offered at least the slim possibility that inmates might work and survive.

By contrast, the Reinhard troika of Belzec, Sobibor, and Treblinka constituted a species of camp wholly new in human history. They were killing centers, and only that. In a macabre misappropriation of the principles of mass production, each existed solely for the purpose of murdering people as rapidly and efficiently as possible. No one was intended to survive.

Jewish children in the ghetto of Lodz are marched to trucks that will carry them to the Chelmno death camp about forty miles to the northwest. From January to June 1942, more than one-fourth of the 200,000 Jews living in Lodz were gassed at Chelmno.

The tunic at left was worn by a Jehovah's Witness at Buchenwald. The SS used purple triangles to mark prisoners regarded as religious deviants. The cap shown above belonged to a prisoner at Majdanek.

The Germans issued a metal identification tag to each prisoner at Majdanek. Although most inmates used wire or rope to tie the tags around their necks or wrists, one prisoner attached his ID number to a soft, less abrasive leather bracelet (above).

Symbols of Damnation

On arriving at a concentration camp, persons not killed outright were stripped of every vestige of freedom and given uniforms that marked them as prisoners of the Reich. Some camps had shops where inmates sewed prison caps, trousers, jackets, and coats from striped cloth. In the final years of the war, however, especially at Majdanek, outfitting inmates was of little importance to the Nazis. Their resources taxed, they either issued clothing stripped from those killed in the gas chambers or had the new arrivals make do with the clothes on their backs. Bright paint was enough to identify an inmate. Cloth badges in various shapes and colors distinguished Jews, Gypsies, homosexuals, Jehovah's Witnesses, political prisoners, asocial prisoners, and habitual criminals. Before the rising tide of inmates swamped the prison system, most of the captives received an identification number that was either tattooed on the forearm or worn on a tag.

The letters *KL* on the back of this jacket *(left)* mark the wearer as a concentration-camp inmate. The letters *OST* on the front *(below)* indicate he was also a forced laborer from the East, while the Star of David inscribed with an *R* shows he was a Russian Jew.

Instead of prison stripes, an inmate at Majdanek wore civilian trousers painted with bright yellow Xs *(left)*. The green triangle indicates the SS classification of habitual criminal.

Jewish men, women, and children arrived by the trainload and were swept up in what an SS physician described as a *laufenden Band* (conveyor belt). They were stripped of their clothing, fed into the gas chambers, and hauled away for burial or burning—typically in less than three hours from arrival. The three camps together could produce more than 25,000 deaths a day.

Decisions by Adolf Hitler led to the creation of the murder factories. No written Führer directives for the final solution survived the war. It is likely that Hitler issued his orders orally, in stages before the invasion of Russia in June 1941: first, to unleash the mobile killer units on the Jews and others in the Soviet Union; then, to eradicate the remainder of European Jewry. Himmler and Göring passed on these orders to subordinates, and the Wannsee conference in Berlin, presided over by Reinhard Heydrich on January 20, 1942, confirmed the details.

As suggested at Wannsee by the representative of the Government General of Poland, that region was given first priority in the process of the final solution. More than one-third of Europe's Jews lived either there or in the regions of western Poland incorporated by the Reich. Poland possessed a good railroad system that could transport the Jews to suitably secluded areas. And the Germans reasoned that many Poles, with their history of anti-Semitism, would look the other way. Heinrich Himmler gave the go-ahead, being careful not to commit his orders to paper.

To direct what would soon become Operation Reinhard, Himmler selected Odilo Globocnik, the thirty-seven-year-old SS chief for the Lublin district in eastern Poland. The son of an Austrian bureaucrat, Globocnik had already dabbled in criminal behavior. After participating in the murder of a Jewish jeweler in Vienna, he had to flee to Germany before the Anschluss. He then served less than a year as the first Nazi gauleiter of Vienna before being dismissed for illegal speculation in foreign currency. His shady past recommended him to Himmler, who grew fond of Globocnik and called him *Globus* (Globe).

If Globocnik lacked the requisite expertise in mass extermination, his SS boss was ready to provide it. Himmler realized that the mass killings staged by his Einsatzgruppen were too unwieldy for the rapid eradication of all the Jews in the Government General. Executions by gunfire were slow, messy, and too public, and they grated on the nerves of the executioners. Himmler had in mind the quiet, efficient methods of killing with carbon-monoxide poisoning perfected in the euthanasia program known as T-4. Much of the program's staff had been out of work since Hitler ended T-4 in August 1941, and Himmler was able to send Globocnik nearly 100 men who had become expert in operating gas chambers.

The foremost practitioner was Christian Wirth, a florid-faced, fifty-six-year-old former chief of the Criminal Police in the city of Stuttgart. Wirth had conducted the first gassing experiments on the incurably insane in 1939 at the euthanasia institution located at Brandenburg an der Havel in Prussia. In 1941, he launched a pilot killing program in Warthegau, a territory in western Poland. Working on behalf of Warthegau's gauleiter, who had gained Himmler's permission to kill 100,000 Jews in his jurisdiction, Wirth set up shop in December at the village of Chelmno, forty miles northwest of the Lodz ghetto.

On the old castle grounds in the village, Wirth installed several motor vans of the type the Einsatzgruppen had experimented with in Russia. In the Ukraine, local people referred to these vans as *dushegubki,* or soul destroyers. They were rigged to direct carbon-monoxide fumes from the engine's exhaust through pipes into a large, hermetically sealed rear cabin to asphyxiate the occupants. The larger vans could accommodate up to 150 occupants, who might be gassed during the drive to the burial grounds some two miles away in a wooded forest, where their corpses were then flung out into open pits. "The most horrifying thing I had ever seen in my life," said Adolf Eichmann, who came out from Berlin to witness the new process. Eichmann was so upset that he neglected to perform his assignment—timing the gassing procedure.

The process did not always go smoothly at Chelmno, although the primitive installation would eventually claim the lives of more than 200,000 Jews and several thousand Gypsies. Wirth found the vans inefficient. The irregular exhaust pressure from the engines sometimes failed to kill quickly enough. Victims often endured a lingering agony, and a few occupants even managed to escape before the fumes took effect. In any event, the camp could process only about 1,000 people a day. To handle the numbers projected for Operation Reinhard, Wirth preferred the old standby he had helped perfect in the euthanasia program—stationary gas chambers.

In early 1942, Wirth poured his ideas for assembly-line killing into the design of Belzec, the prototype of the three death camps. Constructed on the site of a former labor camp, Belzec lay in a remote pine forest some 150 miles southeast of Warsaw, near the Bug River. A main rail line linked the camp to the large Jewish ghetto at Lublin, 75 miles to the north.

Because the camp was intended to take lives, not sustain them, the premises were compact: 162 acres enclosed by barbed wire. The lethal heart of the compound was a small building containing three rooms disguised as shower baths. The source of the carbon monoxide was a 250-horsepower diesel engine taken from an armored car and installed in a shed behind the gas chambers. Wirth decided to generate his own carbon monoxide instead of relying on the commercial bottled variety used in the euthanasia program. He wanted his extermination system to be as self-sufficient as possible.

Wirth tested his equipment and procedures successfully in late February and early March on several hundred Jews, including those who had helped build the camp. Belzec opened officially on March 17, 1942, with a trainload from the Lublin ghetto, and construction was hastened on the other two camps. Both were modeled after Belzec but were slightly larger in area. Sobibor, about 100 miles to the north, started operations during the first week of May. The largest camp, Treblinka, 75 miles northeast of Warsaw, opened on July 23. A few days later, Wirth was named inspector of all three camps. So brutal in manner and deed was Wirth that even his subordinates referred to him as Christian the Terrible.

The camp commanders, all working under Wirth's supervision, were veterans of the euthanasia program. Each camp had a guard contingent of about 100 Ukrainians who were equipped with rifles and leather whips. Many of them were former Soviet soldiers, prisoners of war who had volunteered for service as German *Hilfswillige*, or auxiliaries, and who had no aversion to killing Jews. But the main staff of each camp consisted of approximately thirty SS men—almost all of them T-4 veterans—who had sworn an oath of secrecy to include the "prohibition on photography in the camps." For the Führer, for a bonus of eighteen marks a day, and for frequent home leaves, they were willing to accept the charge that Himmler had given Christian Wirth: to be "superhumanly inhuman."

SS Major Christian Wirth, who pioneered techniques of killing by gas, set up the extermination camp at Chelmno and later administered the Operation Reinhard death camps. In Hitler's chancellery, he was known as the Chief Executioner.

Beginning in the spring and summer of 1942, these remote little camps with their modest staffs received victims from far and wide. While Reinhard was intended primarily to eradicate Jews in the Government General, more than eight percent of the deportees arriving at its three death camps came from other parts of the Reich's vastly expanded dominion, which stretched in a semicircular arc from Norway in the north around through western Europe and into Rumania. Jews from these regions were to be sent to the Reinhard killing centers as well as to the other camps at Majdanek in the Government General and to Chelmno and Auschwitz in the incorporated areas of western Poland.

For Jews from the western countries, the journey to the camps was shrouded in deception. To prevent panic and escape attempts, Eichmann

Jewish men at Chelmno face a lethal ride in a carbon-monoxide gassing van. The vans were the primary means of exterminating the 250,000 Jews of Lodz and the surrounding Warthegau region.

and his minions spread the word that the deportees were bound for labor camps or farms in the East, and usually allowed them to take personal belongings on the trip. Some of the trains were made up of ordinary passenger coaches instead of freight cars, a ploy that heightened the illusion of a peaceful journey to "resettlement in the East." The police stayed out of sight on such trains. Deportees were occasionally asked to purchase tickets, and a conductor maintained the charade by checking the tickets periodically and dutifully tearing off stubs.

In the ghettos of Poland, the deportations to the nearby camps proceeded with far less finesse. Local SS and police leaders, who handled the roundups and transports under the overall coordination of Odilo Globocnik's deputy, Major Herman Höfle, told the deportees that they would be resettled in labor camps farther east, in the Ukraine. Typically, the Nazis gave residents less than a day's notice and then cordoned off the ghetto. Next, SS men, frequently supplemented by Polish police and Ukrainian or Latvian auxiliaries, went into the ghetto streets to make certain the day's deportation quota was met.

Deportation authorities usually sought the cooperation of Jewish leaders. When they approached Moses Merin, chief of the Jewish councils in eastern Upper Silesia in 1941, he agreed to meet their requirements, confidently justifying his compliance with the notion that the sacrifice of some of his people would save the majority. Two years later, Merin sadly told his

dwindling constituency: "I stand in a cage before a hungry and angry tiger. I stuff his mouth with meat, the flesh of my brothers and sisters, to keep him in his cage lest he break loose and tear us all to bits."

The Nazis did not always find Jewish elders so ready to feed the beast. On July 22, 1942, Major Höfle went to the offices of Adam Czerniakow, chairman of the Jewish Council in the huge Warsaw ghetto, to arrange to fill the first trains bound for the newly opened Treblinka death camp. He ordered Czerniakow to supply 6,000 Jews for evacuation to the East that afternoon at 4:00 p.m. and every day thereafter. If Czerniakow failed to comply, the German added, his wife would be the first resident taken hostage and shot. Faced with responsibility for uprooting a community of 350,000 people that already had been drastically reduced by hunger and disease during the previous twenty months, the Jewish leader committed suicide with the cyanide pill he kept in his desk drawer.

Nonetheless, many of the Jews in Poland went willingly to the trains during those early days. In Warsaw, some 20,000 were enticed to volunteer by the offer of a special ration of three kilograms of bread and a kilogram of jam. Far more ghetto residents went in desperation, drawn by the false promise of a better life in a labor camp. Definitive word of the nearby death camps had not yet reached the ghettos, and many occupants "had not the strength to struggle any longer," wrote Emanuel Ringelblum, the chronicler of the Warsaw ghetto.

Later, after the volunteering subsided, scenes of indiscriminate cruelty

Jews in the Polish town of Olkusz are forced to lie facedown in the snow while SD men and local police take their names and select those to be deported. At times during such operations, Jews were made to remain outdoors all night.

marked the roundups in the Polish ghettos. Husbands and wives were separated; mothers were snatched from their babies and taken away. Anyone who resisted or attempted to elude arrest was shot down, along with countless others deemed too old, too sick, or too young. Such decisions were made on the spot, arbitrarily, and were not limited to the jurisdiction of the Government General. In neighboring Warthegau, SS men often conducted ghetto-clearing operations in a half-drunken stupor—the result of an extra daily ration of brandy allotted to see them through their grisly work. During one such action in the Lodz ghetto, hospitals were the target. In the process of deporting more than 2,000 patients, the Germans cleared out the wards by ripping patients from the operating tables and throwing them down the staircases. At one hospital, Ben Edelbaum, a ghetto resident who was searching for his own newborn niece, watched in horror as SS men made sport by hurling infants from an upper-floor window into the bed of a truck parked on the street below. Then Edelbaum heard one of the SS men in the street request permission from his superior

An SS sergeant kicks a Jew climbing aboard a truck in Krakow, while another German soldier grins at the sight. Similar scenes were enacted throughout Poland in 1942 and 1943 as Jews were herded to death camps.

to catch one of those "little Jews" plummeting from the window on the point of his bayonet.

"His superior gave him permission," recalled Edelbaum, "and the young SS butcher rolled up his rifle sleeve and caught the very next infant on his bayonet. The blood of the infant flowed down the knife onto the murderer's arm and into his sleeve. He tried his talent once more, and again he was successful in catching the wailing child on his sharp bayonet. He tried a third time but missed and gave up the whole game, complaining it was getting too 'messy.'"

During the daily roundups in Warsaw, no one was safe, not even those inhabitants who submitted and marched meekly to the trains under the goad of rifle butts and sticks. "He who walked too quickly was shot," a survivor named David Wdowinski recounted later. "He who fell on the way was shot. He who strayed out of line was shot. He who turned his head was shot. He who bent down was shot. He who spoke too loudly was shot. A child who cried was shot."

Unlike victims in the West, who often traveled in relative comfort in passenger coaches, the Polish deportees rode to their deaths cruelly crammed into closed freight cars. As many as 150 people and their belongings frequently were jammed into a single car of these *Sonderzüge*, or special trains, that could decently accommodate fewer than half that number. German trainmen dutifully counted the people packed into each car and chalked the number on the bulkhead.

Deportees traveled without food, water, or toilets. The cars, bolted shut and boarded up to prevent escape, quickly grew suffocating in the heat. The close air teemed with the stench of human bodies and excrement and the quicklime that had been strewn on the floor as a disinfectant. Desperate mothers gave their children urine to quiet their thirst. People worked frantically with hairpins and nails to bore air holes in the car walls. On a train from Warsaw to Treblinka in the summer of 1942, Abraham Kszepicki lay down and stuck his nose through a crack in the floorboards, trying desperately to make contact with fresh air. "People lay on the floor," he recalled, "gasping and shuddering as if feverish, their heads lolling, laboring to get some air into their lungs."

Long delays en route lengthened the ordeal. Journeys that ordinarily might have lasted only a couple of hours frequently extended into a day or more. Although the average distance from ghetto to death camp was no more than seventy-five miles, the final solution overloaded a Polish railroad system already burdened by the requirements of the Russian front. On a typical day, transports with 200 cars carrying as many as 25,000 Jews made their way to the camps. Their progress was impeded by track shutdowns,

Starving women of the Warsaw ghetto gather to volunteer for deportation in exchange for a ration of bread and jam. From July 29 to July 31, 1942, the Jews in Warsaw who accepted such an offer in anticipation of being sent to a work camp met their deaths in a gassing center.

inefficient planning, and bottlenecks at the camps. Treblinka, for example, was not prepared to receive deportees after dark, and two or three incoming trains frequently backed up at the station there during the night.

While the occupants of the cars waited, the horror extended. Screams and moans and cries for water issued from the trains. In search of water for their dying children, women thrust empty bottles fastened to sticks through openings in the car walls and threw out money and gold rings and other jewelry. German guards smashed the bottles, pocketed the money, and shot those who begged for water and anyone who tried to give it to them. "It was forbidden to show even signs of sympathy or pity for the

Jews," said Stanislaw Bohdanowicz, a Pole who lived in Zwierzyniec, on the rail line to Belzec. "The punishment was instant death."

The victims grasped at any straw. If their train stopped at some way station in the dark and they overheard voices speaking Russian, hope flashed—they were certain they had arrived at a labor camp in the Ukraine and were saved. But the voices usually belonged to Ukrainian auxiliaries or other varieties of henchmen who frequently outdid their Nazi masters in brutality. Lithuanian guards, for example, were notorious for shooting blind through the freight cars, swapping bets on how many Jews their bullets would hit. Ukrainian soldiers boarded a Sobibor-bound transport halted in the countryside and rampaged through the cars, robbing the occupants. A Jewish survivor reported that the hurried intruders cut off fingers to get the rings.

A young Austrian soldier encountered a transport of Treblinka-bound Jews during the first summer of deportations and recorded in his diary what he called the "most ghastly scenes." Hubert Pfoch and his infantry company were headed for the Soviet Union when his train stopped in the town of Siedlce on August 21, 1942. On the nearby loading platform, he saw Ukrainian guards pushing into the freight cars Jews who called out that they had been traveling without food or water for two days. "They scream at them, shoot, and hit them so viciously that some of their rifle butts break," he wrote. Trucks came to cart away the corpses that lined the tracks and the platform. Pfoch heard a guard boast that he had killed a mother and her baby "with one shot through both their heads."

Pfoch and his friends urged their commander, a young first lieutenant, to intervene with the SS officer in charge. "He agreed to do it," Pfoch said after the war, "but when he suggested to the SS officer that this outrageous spectacle was unworthy of Germany and German honor, the SS bellowed that if we didn't like it and didn't shut up about it, he'd be glad to 'add a special car to the train for us, and we could join the Jews and warmongers and get to know Treblinka.'"

Thousands of deportees died en route to the camps. They expired of suffocation and dehydration, took their own lives, or were trampled to death in the chaotic cars. The guards who lay atop the cars or perched on the buffers at either end of a car gunned down those passengers who attempted to escape. Poles who lived near the death camps later remembered that the staccato sounds of rifle fire usually signaled the approach of yet another trainload of Jews.

A series of precise orders guided every step of the extermination process from the moment the transports arrived at the three Reinhard death camps. The goal was to kill all but a few of the deportees within two hours.

To achieve this objective, and to prevent any possibility of resistance by the victims, a prescription involving deception, speed, and dehumanization was developed by Christian Wirth at Belzec and then systematically applied at the other camps.

For arrivals from the West, the Germans preserved the illusion of a peaceful journey to a new home. At Treblinka, they created a fake train station to maintain the fiction that the place was merely a transit camp, a stopover en route to better things. There was a station clock with painted hands that never moved. Large signs indicated such nonexistent amenities as a restaurant, ticket office, and telephone, and pointed the direction to "Change for Eastbound Trains." At Sobibor, Jewish inmates who were disguised as porters helped the deportees with their luggage and gave them checks for reclaiming it. The Germans even passed out postcards and

Jews from the Lublin district of Poland ride to the Sobibor death camp in cattle cars of the German National Railroad. Lublin's Jews who were gassed at Sobibor made the one-way journey in various transports, including trucks and relatively luxurious passenger cars.

asked the travelers to write home to Berlin or Amsterdam to report their safe arrival in the East.

The Germans prepared a different reception for deportees from the ghettos of Poland. Less deception was necessary because these arrivals already had been terrorized in the ghetto and on the train—"had already passed through the seven circles of hell," wrote Dov Freiberg, a survivor of Sobibor. As soon as the transport rolled to a stop at the camp, Jewish inmates unbolted the doors and dragged away the corpses littering the cars. Ukrainian guards and SS men hurried out the living occupants with whips, rifles, and incessant shouts and screams. "Everything was done at a lightning speed," recalled Freiberg. "We had no time to think."

This brutal show of force was designed by Wirth to deter escape or resistance by paralyzing the victims' reactions and preventing them from realizing what was going on. Pushing everyone through the process quickly also increased the daily productivity of the camp. And by treating the arrivals brutally and coarsely, as if they were merely livestock, the SS men became immune to humane instincts and found it easier to do their jobs. Franz Stangl, the T-4 veteran who commanded Sobibor and then Treblinka, said later that the point of the dehumanization was "to condition those who had actually had to carry out the policies, to make it possible for them to do what they did."

Soon after arrival at the extermination facility, all deportees were sorted out. A few skilled craftsmen such as carpenters and tailors, along with the strongest-looking young people, were pulled from the ranks to serve on the camp's work force. The selectees did not yet realize that they had been given a reprieve—"born anew," as an SS lieutenant at Sobibor remarked cryptically to one such group.

Then the guards weeded out those who would not be able to keep up with the fast-moving procession of victims. The elderly, invalids, babies, and toddlers were trundled away by Jewish workers—or at Sobibor carried on a special railroad trolley—to the killing ground and burial pits out of earshot of the other Jews. At Treblinka, this area was called the Lazarett, or infirmary. It had a gateway with a Red Cross sign, and its attendants wore phony Red Cross armbands. The executioner, Staff Sergeant August Miete, was known to prisoners as the Angel of Death. He dispatched the too old, too infirm, and too young with a 9-mm pistol aimed at the nape of the neck. They fell into an open pit, where bodies were constantly burning. A survivor of Treblinka, Samuel Rajzman, recalled that "sometimes one could hear infants wailing in the fire."

The final stage in the arrival process was the welcoming speech. Intended to calm even the brutalized deportees from the ghetto, the standard

On August 21, 1942, Austrian soldier Hubert Pfoch, his train delayed en route to the eastern front, secretly photographed the ordeal of a group of Jews at Siedlce, a stop on the rail line to Treblinka. Some 7,000 men, women, and children were being forced into cattle cars (top left). Those who were slow to follow orders were shot or beaten to the ground by Ukrainian guards and left to die (top right). The following day, the 200 or so bodies littering the station area were loaded onto trucks and carted away (bottom).

speech reassured them that this was a transit camp; they would undergo disinfection in the baths to prevent the spread of disease and then be sent on to work in the Ukraine. Christian Wirth himself delivered the words of welcome in the early days at Belzec. The speaker at Sobibor usually was SS Sergeant Hermann Michel, the camp deputy commandant. Known to Jewish inmates as the Preacher for his pleasant voice and slick oratory, Michel wore a white coat to give the impression that he was a physician. His manner and words were so heartening, recalled Ada Lichtman, a Sobibor survivor, that his captive audience "applauded spontaneously and sometimes even danced and sang."

To prepare the deportees for the "baths," the Germans separated the men from the women and children. They herded the groups into barracks—men to the right—and ordered them to strip off their clothing, tie their shoes together for safekeeping, and leave their money, rings, watches, and other valuables. At Sobibor, when time permitted, numbers were handed out as receipts, purportedly for the purpose of reclaiming valuables. Women and girls then had their hair shorn, told it was to stop the spread of head lice; in fact, the hair would be bagged and sent back to the Reich—Treblinka alone exported twenty-five boxcars of it—where it would be made into felt or woven into slipper linings for U-boat crewmen.

By this time, it was impossible for anyone to escape the fate decreed by the Nazis. One day in the undressing hut at Treblinka, an attractive woman tried to step out of the line. She explained to the SS man that she and her two boys were German by birth and not Jewish; they had been put aboard the train by mistake. The papers she carried confirmed her contention. "But she had seen too much and might spread it around," said Jacob Wiernik, who survived the camp. "This woman and her children marched together with the others—to die."

The passageway to the gas chambers at all three camps was known to the staff as The Tube or, in an attempt at black humor, as the Road to Heaven. At Treblinka, it was a road about 15 feet wide bordered on either side by 7-foot-high barbed wire entwined with tree branches so no one could see in or out. About five abreast, led by an SS man, the nude victims were forced to run its 110-yard length, urged on by the guards' whips and clubs, even by jabs of their bayonets. Men went first because the overseers feared they would resist if they saw what was happening to the women.

The victims stood at last waiting their turn in front of the building with the sign "Baths and Inhalation Rooms." By then, they must surely have suspected what awaited them. They had probably heard the rumors that made their way back to the ghettos of Poland during that first spring and summer of 1942, but the stories were unsubstantiated. In any event, recalled Dov Freiberg, who was only fifteen when he was deported to Sobibor on May 12, 1942, "We didn't want to believe." Now those waiting could hear wailing and moans issuing from inside—"just like in a synagogue," remarked a German visitor who put his ear to the outside wall at Belzec. They stood naked, helpless, and resigned, too paralyzed by fear and exhaustion to even think of resistance.

The bathhouse at each camp contained three small gas chambers at first. But these soon proved inadequate to the task, and by early autumn of 1942, the building of additions or new structures more than doubled the capacity. At Treblinka, each chamber measured about four by nine yards and could hold more than 400 victims tightly packed. (The efficient designers, while increasing the square footage, lowered the ceilings a few inches to save on carbon monoxide and to shorten asphyxiation times.) Franz Stangl, the Treblinka commandant, testified after the war that the increased capacity enabled the camp to liquidate 3,000 people in three hours. "When the work lasted for about fourteen hours," he added, "12,000 to 15,000 people were annihilated. There were many days that the work lasted from the early morning until the evening."

The entrance to the new brick bathhouse at Treblinka was flanked by pots of geraniums and other flowers. A large Star of David adorned the front gable, and the entrance was covered with a heavy dark curtain. It had been taken from a synagogue and still bore the Hebrew legend, "This is the gate through which the righteous shall enter." The Jews entered the corridor and were brutally pushed and shoved into the tiled chambers with their fake shower nozzles. Some prayed, others protested with curses. Sometimes they were instructed to raise their arms and pull in their stomachs so that more bodies could be squeezed in. Small children might then be slipped in over the top to make use of the remaining space above their heads. When it was no longer possible to make room for another body, the heavy wooden door was slammed shut.

Then the signal was given to start the diesel engine that would pump carbon monoxide into the chamber. "Ivan, water!" was the cruel signal shouted by the German overseer to a Ukrainian guard at Treblinka. The German overseers prided themselves on the efficiency of their engines, referring to the operators in charge as drivers. At Belzec, a sign on the engine shack next to the bathhouse proclaimed it the Hackenholt Foundation, in honor of the driver, SS Sergeant Lorenz Hackenholt. Not infrequently, however, the engine failed to start. Victims stood in agony inside the chambers for hours; others waited outside, sometimes in below-zero cold so fierce that their naked feet froze to the ground.

But sooner or later, the engines would start up again, and the poisonous fumes would pour into the chamber. The cries and moans rose, then subsided. Then, recalled Rudolf Reder, one of only two Jews to survive Belzec, "came one last terrible shout." A few minutes later, one of the Germans listened at the wall or peered through a small glass peephole, looking for signs of life. At Sobibor, the peepholes were in the roof, and the overseer, Erich Bauer, perched there during the gassing. The all-clear signal was usually given about thirty minutes after the engine was switched on. The guards flung open trapdoors opposite the entrances, and the Jewish inmates of the so-called death brigade started the ghastly task of clearing the gas chambers.

An SS man, Karl Schluch, who sometimes supervised the clearing process at Belzec, recalled the scene: "The Jews inside the gas chambers were densely packed. This is the reason that the corpses were not lying on the floor but were mixed up in disorder in all directions, some of them kneeling, according to the amount of space they had. I could see that the lips and tips of the noses were a bluish color. Some of them had their eyes closed, others' eyes rolled."

A visitor to Belzec, SS Lieutenant Kurt Gerstein, described it this way: "The people were still standing like columns of stone, with no room to fall or lean. Even in death you could tell the families, all holding hands. It was difficult to separate them while emptying the room for the next batch. The bodies were tossed out, blue, wet with sweat and urine, the legs smeared with excrement and menstrual blood. Two dozen workers were busy checking mouths, which they opened with iron hooks. Dentists knocked out gold teeth, bridges, and crowns with hammers."

The original method of disposal was burial. Driven mercilessly by their overseers, Jews of the death brigade dragged or carried their brethren to enormous ditches 180 feet long, 45 feet wide, and 20 feet deep. Treblinka had hand-pushed trolleys for this purpose, but they had to be abandoned because the inmates were so harried that the corpse-laden carts kept jumping the tracks. In fact, the burial process soon proved inadequate. At Treblinka, the killing during the first month of operation simply outpaced the camp's disposal capabilities, and corpses were stacked everywhere. At

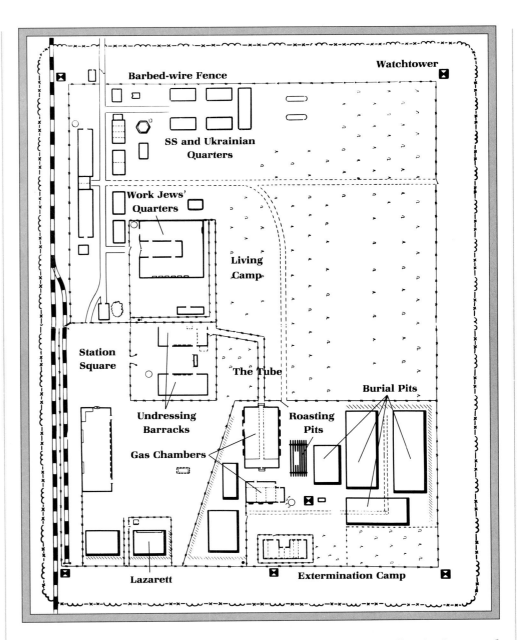

More than 700,000 Jews rode past the depot of Treblinka *(above)* on their way to oblivion. Trainloads of victims entered the camp *(right)* and debarked at Station Square. The elderly, the sick, and very young children were taken directly to the Lazarett, a phony clinic, where they were shot. The rest went to barracks to undress and have their heads shaved. They were then herded along a path called The Tube to the gas chambers. SS men and Ukrainian auxiliaries lived at the camp's northern end. Work Jews lived where they labored, in either the Extermination Camp or the Living Camp.

Sobibor and Belzec, difficulties developed after burial. Swollen by heat and putrefaction in the mass graves, the bodies heaved so violently that they split the ground, creating a terrible stench as well as a health menace.

Himmler, in the meantime, determined to do a better job of covering up the traces of the final solution. He assigned Paul Blobel, a former commander of one of his mobile killer groups, to find the most efficient means of destroying the evidence. Working at Chelmno during the summer of 1942 under the code name *Sonderaktion* 1005 (Special Command 1005), Blobel and a small staff began exhuming victims of the gas vans there. They experimented with incendiary bombs but finally settled on cremation over enormous open fireplaces. Any bones that remained after burning were reduced in a special bone-crushing machine. Ashes and bone fragments were then buried in the pits from which the bodies had been disinterred.

Blobel's efficient new system for disposing of bodies was gradually adopted at the three camps despite the grudging opposition of the chief of Operation Reinhard, Odilo Globocnik. In the presence of the Führer himself, Globocnik remarked that the Reich ought to take visible pride in

its work. Instead of cremating bodies to cover up the killings, he said, "We ought, on the contrary, to bury bronze tablets stating that it was we who had the courage to carry out this gigantic task." Sobibor was the first to burn its victims, beginning in autumn 1942. Shortly thereafter, in December, Belzec shut down its gas chambers for good and began exhuming the estimated 600,000 bodies buried there. Treblinka did not adopt cremation until March 1943, after a visit from Himmler.

Treblinka's burning operations were the busiest, biggest, and best documented by eyewitnesses. Some 700,000 corpses had to be unearthed and cremated while, simultaneously, bodies fresh from the gas chambers had to be disposed of. As in the other camps, mechanical excavators dug up the corpses, six or eight to the scoop, and dumped them on the ground. Teams of Jewish prisoners then transferred them on stretchers to gigantic steel grids that could hold as many as 3,000 stacked-up bodies. Known to the Germans as a "roaster," the 100-foot-wide grid consisted of a half-dozen railroad rails, resting on three rows of 28-inch-high concrete posts.

Brushwood placed underneath the grid served as the kindling. The bodies were sometimes doused with gasoline, but then the SS men made a discovery. They found that women burned more rapidly than men because females possess more subcutaneous fat. The fire did nicely without gasoline if female bodies were properly arranged in the bottom layer. From female and male, old corpses and new, the flames leaped above the pyres around the clock, and the smell of flesh burning at the rate of 7,000 bodies a day could be detected for miles around.

While teams of Jewish inmates reduced the bones to particles and

Gypsies *(left)* photographed in 1940 at the Belzec labor camp betray no sense of distress at their status as conscripted laborers. By the spring of 1942, Belzec had become a killing camp where more than a half-million Jews and several thousand Gypsies were eventually gassed or shot, including the woman *(below)* who faces execution beside the crumpled form of a fellow victim.

dumped the ashes into the open pits from which the bodies had been exhumed, others processed the plunder taken from the victims. All the clothing, jewelry, money, watches, eyeglasses, baby carriages, bedding, briefcases, and other belongings had to be cleaned and sorted; the Jewish

star had to be removed from clothing and the seams checked for hidden valuables. Currency and articles of value, including dental gold, went to the German central bank. Other items were sold or distributed free to such beneficiaries as Ethnic Germans and SS men and their families.

By official accounting, more than $70 million in money and goods was confiscated from Jews at the three Reinhard killing centers. The total did not include all the camp pilferage by the German and Ukrainian staff members who, in defiance of Himmler's strict orders against personal gain, discovered that personal profit could be made from mass murder. They, in turn, enriched some of the Poles in the surrounding countryside as they sought entertainment and diversion from the daily grind.

Those Jews who were selected for work details rather than for the gas chambers were thereafter bound together with their German overseers in the business of mass extermination. These so-called work Jews did all the physical labor that enabled the camps to function. The initial practice of liquidating them after a day or two of labor proved to be inefficient, and the camp administrators soon created semipermanent work forces of as many as 1,000 inmates.

There were such specialists as the *Friseurs*, or hair cutters, and the *Goldjuden*, or gold Jews, who sorted the valuables, including the gold extracted by the so-called dentists. Craftsmen such as tailors, carpenters, and shoemakers were called court Jews because the staff relied on them for personal services and because they frequently were accorded special privileges. At Treblinka, the teams of specialists assigned to various steps in the killing cycle, from platform workers to the burial details, were so efficiently organized that they had their own color-coded badges or armbands. Each work group was supervised by a Jewish Kapo (from the Italian *capo*, for chief or boss), typically chosen by the Germans for his willingness to punish his own people when so ordered.

Daily life in the camps was so harsh that the reprieve from death provided by selection as a work Jew seldom exceeded a few months. Food usually consisted of a watery turnip soup, sawdust bread, and whatever inmates could pilfer from packages carried by victims on the incoming trains. Dysentery, typhus, and skin diseases of all kinds were epidemic. Prisoners were flogged and sometimes shot. The slightest infraction, or merely an overseer's whim, would suffice to justify such punishments: if a Jew did not run fast enough, or failed to salute properly, or, said a survivor of Belzec, "if an SS man didn't like the look on someone's face." Work Jews especially dreaded the roll calls, which were held as many as three times a day. A roll call was often the occasion for a new selection in which the

In an attempt to eradicate traces of its crimes, the SS at Treblinka use a crane to exhume 700,000 bodies from mass graves in 1943. Jewish prisoners carried the corpses to a pit where up to 3,000 were cremated at one time.

Germans weeded out anyone with signs of sickness or weakness—even the marks of a recent German-inflicted flogging. Those selected were liquidated and replaced with new arrivals.

"The selection was a constant threat, like a drawn sword over our heads," wrote Abraham Kszepicki, a worker who escaped from Treblinka only to die resisting the Germans in the Warsaw ghetto. "In the morning, we would awaken before the signal and arrange our appearance to look better. Never, even in the best of times, did we shave so often as in Treblinka. Every morning, everyone would shave and wash his face in eau de cologne taken from the bundles left by [dead] Jews. Some powdered their faces and even rouged their lips, pinched their cheeks till they were rosy, and all this to gain another few days of life, perhaps a few weeks, who knew?"

Such was the mind-numbing dread and the exhausting routine of the camps that survivors found it nearly impossible to differentiate the behavior of the SS men who ran them. Were they truly sadistic in nature or merely ordinary people loyally carrying out Himmler's orders to be "superhumanly inhuman"? Surprisingly, several Jewish survivors later singled out at least two staff members for small kindnesses such as providing extra food: Erwin Lambert at Treblinka and Karl Ludwig, who served at both Sobibor and Treblinka. But the list of Germans whose brutal behavior seemed to exceed the call of duty was infinitely longer, filled with men like Kurt Bolender. A Jewish inmate at Sobibor, Moshe Bahir, described one of

Bolender's favorite pastimes: "On his way to lunch, he was in the habit of passing by the main gate and swinging a whip with all his strength upon the heads of the Jews who went through—this to increase his appetite for the meal that awaited him."

An extreme difference in attitude and behavior was evident between Franz Stangl, the Treblinka commandant, and his deputy, Lieutenant Kurt Franz. Stangl was an Austrian who had been a master weaver before taking up work as a police investigator and then joining the Nazi euthanasia program. A devoted family man, a Catholic who went to mass on Christmas and Easter and seemed not to be sadistic in temperament, he had little direct contact with his victims. He was rarely seen by them except when he showed up impeccably dressed in white linen riding clothes upon the arrival of a new transport. He said later he regarded the deportees as

inhuman "cargo—I rarely saw them as individuals. It was always a huge mass." He claimed to have taken pride in overseeing the destruction of hundreds of thousands of people, although he drank brandy every night to help him sleep. "That was my profession," he said after the war. "I enjoyed it. It fulfilled me."

Stangl's second in command, Kurt Franz, on the other hand, was described by witnesses as a "sadist of exquisite cruelty." A veteran of the Buchenwald concentration camp and of the euthanasia program, the youthful-looking Franz maintained such an appearance of baby-faced innocence that prisoners nicknamed him *Lalka*, Polish for "doll." A former boxer, he liked to use inmates as punching bags. He once challenged a prisoner who was a former professional prizefighter and then killed him with a pistol concealed in his boxing glove. He also seemed to take pleasure in throwing babies against a wall. But Franz was perhaps most notorious for his dog Barry, whom he trained to attack the genitals of his victims. A mixed breed with St. Bernard predominating, Barry was as big as a small pony, but when Franz was not around to incite him, the dog turned out to be lazy and harmless.

There was another side to life in the camps. The SS overseers encouraged entertainments among the work Jews. They promoted love affairs, staged mock marriages between inmates, allowed chess and card games, and at Belzec, arranged soccer matches on Sundays between the staff and the

work Jews. "When they lost a game," said one of the two Belzec survivors, "they had no complaints." Every camp had a small musical ensemble to help drown out the tumult of the killing and to entertain the staff. The most ambitious orchestra played at Treblinka, where the director, Artur Gold, a prominent prewar conductor in Warsaw, had been plucked naked from the gas chamber procession. Dressed in special blue-and-white suits, Gold's ten-man group performed at plays, operettas, and other special events. Their playing was a regular feature of the evening roll call, which ended with the inmates singing the Treblinka anthem, a hymn in praise of "work, obedience, and duty," with music by Gold.

As the Germans well knew, these diversions helped prevent the inmates from thinking about escape or resistance. Smooth operation of the camps depended on the passivity of the Jews, and the overseers became particularly watchful in early 1943 as the number of transports dwindled. Himmler had ordered the liquidation of all the Jews in the Government General of Poland by the end of 1942, and most of this goal had been achieved. Belzec already had shut down its gas chambers, and the pace of killing at the other death camps had slowed. Only the need to dispose of some transports from Holland, the Balkans, and the Bialystok area of the annexed part of Poland kept Treblinka and Sobibor functioning. The overseers knew the days of the camps were numbered—and that the work Jews might begin to look for ways to avoid the fate that awaited them at the end.

Resistance in the camps began as isolated acts of desperation. At Treblinka in September 1942, a work Jew named Meir Berliner stepped out of line at evening roll call and plunged a knife into the back of Max Bialas, mortally wounding the SS man. The assassin of Max Bialas died along with some 150 of his fellow work Jews, who were shot in reprisal. Then, in December 1942, scores of youths being deported from the Bialystok area resisted the killing process at Treblinka. One tossed a grenade; others attacked the Ukrainians and Germans with fists and knives. The Jews paid a price for such resistance: The young men from Bialystok were shot or gassed.

In scores of instances, work Jews, individually or in small groups, attempted to escape. They hid in the stacks of clothing being shipped out in freight cars or slipped over the compound fence at night. And after definitive word of the true fate of deportees reached the ghettos of Poland during the autumn of 1942, thousands of Jews either attempted to elude the Nazi roundups or jumped from the trains destined for the death camps.

Only a handful of these escapees from camp, ghetto, and train survived to make their way to freedom or to join friendly partisan units belonging to the Polish underground. Many must have felt like Matti Drobless, who at the age of twelve escaped from the Warsaw ghetto along with his fourteen-year-old sister and nine-year-old brother. "We thought we were the only Jews left in the world," he said later. "We would survive, but I believed that we would be the sole survivors. We never met another Jew in our wanderings through the forest."

Most of the Poles whom the Jewish fugitives encountered proved to be indifferent or altogether hostile. They were influenced by centuries of

Portraits of the Hopeless

"A transport departs for Sobibor. We are next to the tracks, dressed in rail workers' uniforms so as not to be suspected as runaway Jews. In the distance bodies are burning."

Among the surviving artifacts that bear witness to the suffering of those caught up in the final solution are the drawings of one Joseph Richter. Hurriedly penciled on old newspapers or Nazi propaganda posters, the sketches depict the plight of Jewish and Polish prisoners in and around the Sobibor killing camp near Lublin in 1943. Richter's subjects are hauntingly clear, but the artist himself remains a mystery. Nothing is known of his life, nationality, or career, only that

he left eighteen sketches with a farmer near Chelm in the Sobibor area, but never returned to retrieve them. Perhaps he was a Polish rail worker, a Jew with false identity papers, or an escapee from Sobibor. It is believed that he joined the partisan movement after 1943 and likely died in the fighting.

The visual testaments shown here are captioned with Richter's own words, found scrawled on the back of each portrayal along with his signature and the date.

"Jews are waiting for the train from Chelm. They have been brought from the camp by Ukrainian and SS troops to collect luggage."

"Sobibor. A high wall plaited from branches hides the gas chambers. A train is hidden on the sidetrack behind the wall. The transport has to be divided in two. Time of unloading: twenty minutes."

"At the station in Uhrusk [near Sobibor] an old Jewish woman ran away; she had her right arm broken. German *Grenzschutz* did not want to kill her. It was done by the Ukrainian police. One is digging a grave near the railway; another waits to shoot her. She begs: 'Only a little vodka.' "

Polish anti-Semitism, fear of German reprisals, and the promise of German rewards for information. The fugitives, feeling insecure in the countryside, tended to find their way back to the ghetto. So many escapees from deportation trains found refuge in the Zolkiew ghetto that inhabitants there coined nicknames for them: "jumpers" or "parachutists." But the fugitives faced the same problem all over again when their ghetto was selected for additional deportations or outright liquidation. Giza Petranker escaped from one transport en route to Belzec, found refuge in Zolkiew, and then had to jump another train when that ghetto's occupants were deported to Belzec.

In the spring of 1943, Jewish resistance, which had been limited to isolated acts against the Germans, exploded in what remained of the Warsaw ghetto. Once Europe's largest, the ghetto had been reduced to about 70,000 residents during the previous autumn. In a period of two months, more than 250,000 Jews had been deported from there to Treblinka, where they were gassed at the rate of 4,000 a day.

The desperate hope to escape, survive, and bear witness gave new meaning to life in the two Reinhard death camps still in operation during that spring of 1943. By the time transports carrying deportees from Warsaw reached Treblinka in May with news of the insurrection, the work Jews there already had organized their own resistance group. During the following weeks, the new Treblinka underground prepared a careful plan. The plotters, more than sixty prisoners in all, were organized into teams with special assignments for the day of the uprising. Grenades and rifles would be taken from the camp arsenal—a Jewish locksmith had made a duplicate key—and then quietly distributed to the teams from a handcart. The worker responsible for daily decontamination of the camp would put gasoline in his sprayer instead of disinfectant in order to prepare wooden buildings for the torch.

Launching of the revolt was repeatedly delayed. But prisoners sensed that the camp's business—and hence their own lives—would soon come to an end. Zero hour was finally set for 4:30 p.m. on August 2, 1943. Everything looked good: The camp commander, Franz Stangl, was drinking with a friend in his quarters, and it was such a hot day that his brutal deputy, Kurt Franz, had taken a group of twenty German and Ukrainian staff members to swim in the Bug River.

But unforeseen circumstances triggered the revolt prematurely. An SS sergeant became suspicious and had to be shot about thirty minutes before the scheduled beginning. The premature start threw the underground's precision timing into turmoil and prevented distribution of all the stolen weapons. Nonetheless, the insurgents wounded one German, killed or wounded a half-dozen Ukrainians, and set ablaze many of the buildings, though not the gas chambers. Most of the camp's 850 workers managed to break out and enjoy a taste of freedom, however brief. The Germans brought in a trainload of reinforcements to track down the fugitives, and only about 100 of them eluded the dragnet. Fewer still survived the war. But these few score could be thankful for the timeliness of their uprising. Treblinka received its last trainload of deportees, a transport from the Bialystok ghetto, on August 19, only seventeen days after the revolt.

At Sobibor, meanwhile, a revolt committee thrashed about ineffectually during the first part of 1943. The necessity for action took on new urgency in June when the 600 workers who had remained at Belzec completed the burning of old corpses there and were transferred to Sobibor and shot. The slowdown in transports arriving at Sobibor indicated that a similar fate awaited its workers. The camp's inmates hatched a number of abortive escape schemes that summer, including separate plots to poison the food of the SS staff, bribe Ukrainian guards to bring in trucks, set fire to the clothing warehouse, and construct tunnels. The Germans discovered one of the tunnels and shot 150 prisoners in reprisal. The inmates, it seemed, lacked a leader with the ability to plan and execute a campwide escape.

The leader Sobibor needed arrived in late September on a transport of 2,000 Jews from the Russian city of Minsk. Lieutenant Alexander Pechersky was one of about 100 men on the train who had been taken prisoner while serving in the Red Army. Pechersky already had attempted unsuccessfully to escape from a prisoner-of-war camp and was ready to try again. Within a week of his arrival at Sobibor, he had so impressed the other prisoners with his unquenchable pride and assertiveness that they made him chief of their underground with the charge of organizing a mass escape.

Pechersky scheduled the uprising for October 14. It was none too soon, for the last train of deportees to be gassed at Sobibor arrived on the 11th. At the time of the attack, a dozen or so SS men were on vacation, including the camp commandant. Pechersky's timetable called for getting rid of the key members of the remaining staff. Beginning at 3:30 p.m., SS officials were lured under various pretexts, one by one, to the tailor shop, shoemaker's, and other workshops and warehouses. One was summoned for a fitting; another was drawn to a corner of the clothing warehouse by the promise of a nice coat. A team of ax-wielding prisoners waiting at each station attacked and killed the Germans. By 5:00 p.m., eight SS men lay dead, telephone and electric wires had been cut, and the Jewish stove repairman had smuggled six rifles out of the Ukrainian barracks—all without alerting the remaining members of the camp staff.

The second phase of Pechersky's plan was even more daring. It called

The Warsaw ghetto lies in a heap of rubble, having been destroyed by the Germans in retaliation for the uprising by its Jewish occupants in the spring of 1943. The Nazis similarly obliterated all other ghettos in occupied Poland before being driven out of the country by the Red Army.

for the camp's 600 prisoners to assemble routinely for evening roll call as if nothing had happened. They would then march out the main gate before the now-leaderless Ukrainian guards realized something was amiss. But as the prisoners gathered, excitement rushed through the ranks; a German noticed the pushing and jostling, intervened, and was struck down by hatchets. Inmates tried to break into the armory for additional arms, but failed. In a matter of moments, Pechersky and other leaders lost control of the revolt. Panic-stricken prisoners, under fire from the Ukrainians and surviving Germans, broke through the fences and into the lethal minefields beyond, climbing over the blown-up bodies of their comrades. They had left behind at least 13 dead enemies, including 11 SS men.

In the resulting confusion, it was morning before the Germans could organize a full-scale search aided by aerial reconnaissance. They hunted down and shot most of the escapees. Perhaps 70 of the fugitives from Sobibor survived the war, including the intrepid Pechersky and a half-dozen or so other Red Army veterans who made their way across the Bug River and joined Soviet partisans.

The trouble at Treblinka and Sobibor so alarmed Himmler that he ordered the elimination of another potential source of insurrection. In early November, some 42,000 Jews being kept as slave laborers at other kinds of camps in eastern Poland were shot.

Thus did Operation Reinhard come to an official end. Some 1.7 million people had been annihilated in the three extermination camps during a period of nineteen months, most of them in 1942. The Jewish ghettos had been eliminated, and scarcely any Jews still lived in the Government General. The new, improved gas chambers at Auschwitz could now meet the needs for exterminating Jews from the rest of occupied Europe.

At Himmler's orders, painstaking care was taken to obliterate every trace of the Reinhard death camps during that autumn. The buildings were razed and plowed under, and grass, lupine, and pine trees were planted. Ukrainians were paid to live there with their families—to farm and to guard the premises from neighboring Poles who had already dug up the refurbished earth at Belzec looking for gold and other valuables. At Treblinka, the farmer was a former guard; his house was made of bricks taken from the dismantled gas chambers.

"This is a page of glory in our history that has never been written and that is never to be written," Himmler had confidently told a group of high-ranking officers ten days before the uprising at Sobibor. But scores of desperate fugitives from Treblinka and then Sobibor had fought back, found refuge in the forests of eastern Europe, and now lived to bear witness against what Himmler's minions could not bury. ✚

Annihilation of a Ghetto

On April 19, 1943, Heinrich Himmler launched an operation to annihilate the Warsaw ghetto. The timing was deliberate: Hitler would be fifty-four years old on the following day, and the SS chief wanted to close another chapter in the final solution as a birthday gift for his Führer. Early on the 19th, a column of SS troops supported by armored cars and small tanks rolled into the ghetto and down Zamenhoff Street to round up the 60,000 Jews who lived there.

Himmler's birthday surprise backfired when his SS phalanx was ambushed by a band of Jewish guerillas firing small arms and hurling homemade grenades and Molotov cocktails from doorways, alleys, and rooftops. Six hours later, the stunned Germans withdrew. The SS returned the following day with a force of more than 2,000 men, but Jewish resistance was fierce, and what was planned as a three-day roundup evolved into a bitter month-long campaign.

Untrained and outnumbered three to one, the ghetto fighters knew they were doomed to fail, but they were determined to make the Nazis bleed for every inch of ground. The uprising was undertaken "solely for death with dignity, and without the slightest hope of victory in life," wrote Alexander Donat, one of the survivors.

SS General Jürgen Stroop *(fourth from right)*, commander of the Warsaw operation, watches with approval as ghetto buildings burn. He was subsequently executed as a war criminal.

SS troops search for concealed weapons in the clothing of Jewish workers at a German armament firm located in the Warsaw ghetto. White tags mark the men as German employees.

A Jewish man leaps from a blazing apartment building into a pile of bodies below *(right)*. "The omnipotent flames were now able to accomplish what the Germans could not do," partisan leader Marek Edelman wrote. "Thousands of people perished in the conflagration."

"A Great Blazing Furnace"

Faced with the prospect of a bitter struggle for the control of every building, General Stroop ordered his men to put the torch to the ghetto. Moving methodically from house to house, the German engineers drenched wooden floors and staircases with gasoline and then stood back to watch the flames consume the neighborhood.

"The ghetto became a great blazing furnace, with no fresh air and suffocating heat and fetid odors," one of the residents recalled in vivid terms. "The hiss of fire and the collapsing of buildings drowned out the sounds of gunfire, although from time to time the wind carried a human moan or distant scream."

Silhouetted against the rubble, German artillerymen move into action. SS artillery units pulverized the gutted structures to ensure that no Jews could hide in the ruins.

On April 22, an SS assault team patrols the streets of the ghetto (left), ready to gun down any Jews who might try to flee their burning quarters. Stroop explained that torching the ghetto was the "only and ultimate way to defeat the rabble and scum of the earth and bring them aboveground."

The Battle of the Bunkers

With their dwellings aflame, thousands of Jews moved underground into makeshift bunkers, subterranean passageways, and sewers in order to evade capture. One partisan described two days in a sewer with water up to his lips: "Every minute, someone else lost consciousness. Thirst was the worst handicap. Some even drank the thick, slimy sewer water. Every second seemed like months."

When Stroop and his men attempted to flood the sewer system, the Jews thwarted them by blowing up the control valves. The Germans then resorted to tossing smoke bombs and poisonous gas grenades into the underground labyrinth to annihilate the resistants. Informers and trained dogs were employed to sniff out other bunker dwellers. The few survivors were promptly shipped to concentration camps.

On April 27, two resistance fighters surrender to the SS. Other Jews would hold out for an additional three weeks, staving off the Nazis until all strength was gone.

Frightened Jews evacuate their bunker under the ready gun of Josef Blösche (*above, right*), a guard called Frankenstein by ghetto residents because of the atrocities he inflicted on them.

An SS officer aims his pistol at a Jew emerging from an underground bunker. A stickler for documentation and detail, Stroop kept a running tally of the 631 bunkers that were destroyed during the fighting.

Some of the last Jews of Warsaw are marched to the train station for deportation *(right)*. Thousands of others, like this family lying dead in the rubble *(inset)*, perished within the ghetto walls of starvation, typhus, gunshot wounds, or the inhalation of chlorine gas.

The Failed Insurrection

On May 16, Stroop announced that the insurrection had ended. "The Jewish Quarter of Warsaw is no more!" he triumphantly reported to his superiors. It had taken the SS four weeks to clear a neighborhood that measured 1,000 by 300 yards, covering about 2.4 percent of the city's area. To commemorate this "grand operation," Stroop blew up Warsaw's Great Synagogue, an architectural landmark that stood outside the ghetto walls. He reported his losses as 16 dead and 85 wounded, a blatant understatement that accounted for only a fraction of the actual casualties.

Most of the Jewish survivors eventually died in concentration camps. Of the original 750 armed insurgents, fewer then 100 managed to elude the Germans.

Beyond the Auschwitz Station

The Germans forbade photographing the horrors of their death camps. In the spring of 1944, however, SS Sergeant Bernhard Walter was for unknown reasons allowed to take pictures of a trainload of Hungarian Jews being sent to their doom in the gas chambers of Birkenau, the killing department of Auschwitz. Discovered by a Jewish survivor at the end of the war, the photograph album is the only known visual record of

Looking uncertain and fearful about what lies ahead, Hungarian Jews debark at Birkenau.

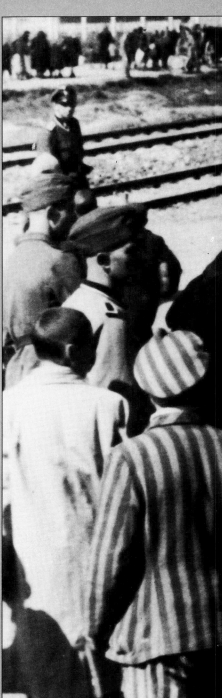

Men are separated from women and children, unaware that most partings were forever.

the factory-like process that rendered newly arrived Jews into Birkenau's final product, ashes of the dead.

A selection of the photographs, shown here and on the following pages, begins with SS men receiving the victims on a rail spur built especially to expedite the extermination of Hungary's Jews at Birkenau. In an exercise called the *Selektion*, an SS man unceremoniously directed all but the sturdiest arrivals to turn left, to join the long line shown at the top of the photograph below. They were told it was the line to the baths; in fact, it led to the gas chamber. Those who were sent to the right faced a short period of abuse, privation, and crushing work as slave laborers until they, too, died or were killed. The Nazis operated the facility with mind-numbing dispatch—Jews not reserved for labor might be dead within two hours of leaving the train.

With a swing of his cane, an SS man *(center, rear, right arm extended)* **consigns an old woman and a toddler to death.**

End of the Line

By the corrupt calculus of efficiency at Birkenau, able-bodied prisoners might briefly be exploited for their muscle power or special skills, but old people and young children and their mothers offered no such benefit to the Reich. For them, there was no interval before death.

When Auschwitz had more slave laborers than it could use—as hap-pened during the deportation of the Hungarian Jewish communi-ty—even a robust constitution could not always save a Jew from extermination. No one bothered with selection; entire trainloads were simply waved to the line for the gas chamber. A Jewish doctor who survived Auschwitz reported that the morning after a particularly heavy day at the gas chambers, he noticed that the lightning rods atop the chimneys of the crematoriums were bent and twisted, so much heat had been generated by the thousands of burning bodies.

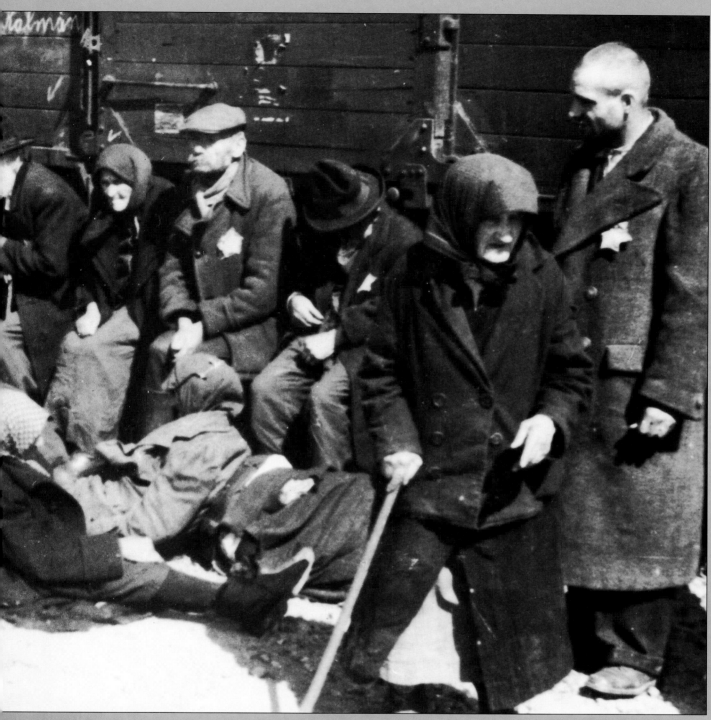

Enfeebled by the ordeal of their two-and-a-half-day journey in a packed and suffocating boxcar, some of the old people at trackside are unable to stand for the selection process. Later, they will be taken to the gas chamber in a dump truck and tipped onto the ground like sacks of coal.

An old woman with an infant and the three other carefully dressed children in her care trudge unknowingly to the gas chambers at Birkenau.

Reprieve without Mercy

Those spared immediate death often faced a worse fate. First, their clothes and belongings were taken away, their heads were shaved, and they were deloused; then, a number was tattooed on their arms. The whole time they were goaded by curses and blows from SS guards.

Then they learned Birkenau's dark secret: The loved ones they had last seen on the train platform, along with multitudes of other Jews, were now dead and their bodies had been consumed by flames.

The survivors' shock and grief were soon numbed by the brutal conditions of camp life. Inhuman labor, savage abuse, starvation, and the threat of execution for the merest infraction condemned the prisoners to an average of three months of hellish existence before it was their turn in the gas chamber.

Shorn of their dignity as well as their hair, female slave workers parade from the delousing station to their compound.

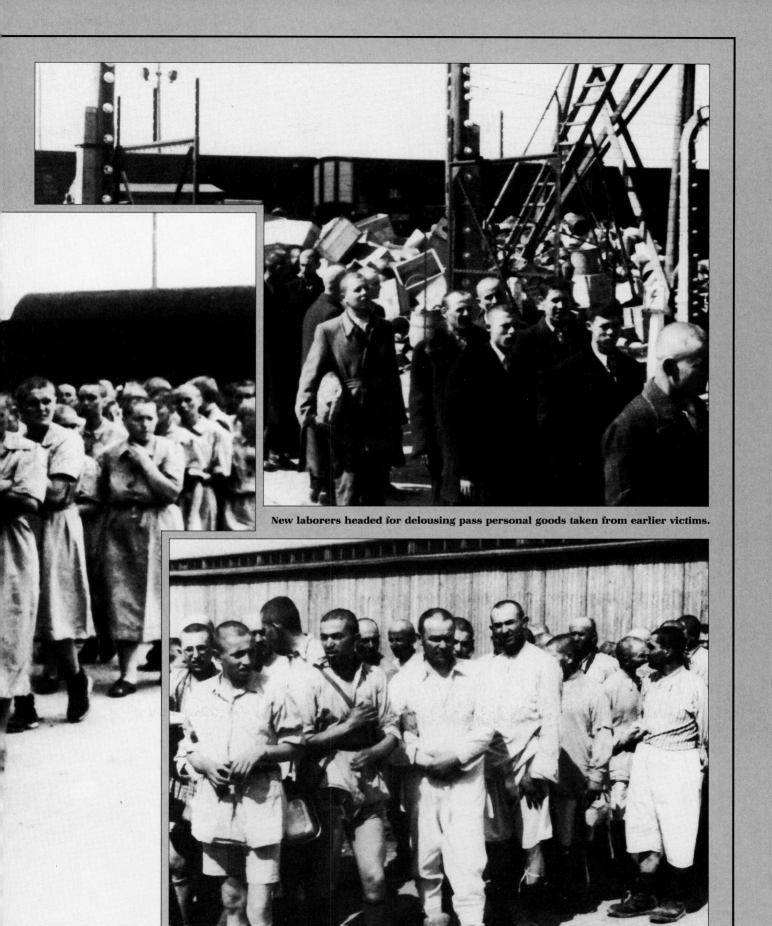

New laborers headed for delousing pass personal goods taken from earlier victims.

Jewish men chosen for work at Auschwitz stand physically and emotionally bereft.

Plunder from the Victims

Each family deported to Auschwitz was permitted to take 50 kilograms—about 110 pounds—of luggage for their "resettlement." The resulting avalanche of personal property was confiscated and hauled to a corner of Birkenau that came to be called "Canada"—an allegorical symbol of storybook riches compared to the want and degradation of the rest of the camp.

Ironically, the sorting and handling of the plunder was strictly off-limits to SS personnel and even to non-Jewish prisoners. Only Jews were allowed to perform this privileged work, on the cold-blooded premise that because no Jew would leave the camp alive, none had any motivation to skim valuables. Despite this precaution, guards and inmates alike managed to rake off a share of the spoils, including money, jewelry, gold, clothing, cigars, and fancy foods. One female "Canada" worker donned a fellow prisoner's worn-out, useless shoes every morning and exchanged them at work for a good pair, which she would wear back to the barracks at night. Others would bring food for their starving barracks mates.

Male prisoners pick through the residue of lost communities of Jews. By 1944, a two-year backlog of unsorted goods had piled up, some of it rotting outdoors.

Female workers—young, well-dressed, and healthy—cull valuables from a heap of booty. Much that was precious to starving inmates was crushed underfoot.

The Threshold of Darkness

Perhaps three-fourths of the Jews in each transport were taken directly to the gas chambers and crematoriums. But the accelerated deportations of Hungarian Jews—which were intended to liquidate that community before the country was liberated by the onrushing Soviet army—overtaxed the killing system. Victims like the group at right, fresh from the trains, could not be sent immediately to their deaths. Kept calm by promises of a shower, something to drink, and assignment to their quarters, most were unable to admit to themselves—or even to imagine—the horrific meaning of the foul black smoke rising from the chimneys and the acrid, sweet smell in the air.

An agitated prisoner, possibly sensing the truth about the destiny of her group, is restrained. In the background is one of Birkenau's gas chambers.

In the birch grove that gave the death camp its name, apprehensive but still-hopeful Jews wait at the last stop before being sent into the killing facility.

The Ultimate Murder Factory

During the summer of 1941, an SS captain named Rudolf Höss found himself with what was later described as a "difficult and onerous" problem. Höss was the commander of Auschwitz, then a small and obscure concentration camp in a swampy area of Upper Silesia, a region Germany had annexed from the southwest corner of occupied Poland. Since its opening in June 1940, Auschwitz had served as a penal camp for Polish political prisoners. But then Höss was summoned to Berlin by his chief, Heinrich Himmler, and entrusted with a new and highly secret mission. Auschwitz, Himmler told him, had been designated as a principal center for the extermination of the Jews.

The enormity of this assignment elicited no evident moral qualms in Höss. He was the ideal SS man, a loyal and unquestioning servant. He had grown up in Baden-Baden in southwest Germany with such a strong sense of duty that his father, a shopkeeper and devout Roman Catholic, had wanted him to be a priest. But the outbreak of World War I induced Höss at the age of fifteen to enlist in the army, where two years later he became the youngest noncommissioned officer in the German armed forces. A member of the paramilitary Freikorps after the war, he served five years in prison for his role in a right-wing political assassination—the only murder he would ever commit with his own hands. He then joined the SS in 1934 and worked his way up the career ladder in the Dachau and Sachsenhausen concentration camps.

Proud to be singled out by his chief, Höss nonetheless fretted about the practical mechanics of mass extermination. He was convinced that the carbon-monoxide process pioneered in the euthanasia program and later adopted at the other death camps was impracticable for large-scale killing, and he looked around for something more efficient. In September 1941, soon after Höss's meeting with Himmler, one of his deputies at Auschwitz began experimenting with a possible solution.

Secret orders had come down to execute a group of Soviet prisoners of war transferred from other camps. Höss's deputy crammed them into a

Electrically charged barbed-wire fences marked "Danger: High Voltage" enclose the stone buildings of Auschwitz I. A number of desperate inmates committed suicide by hurling themselves on the wire.

block of underground detention cells and tossed in pellets of a substance called Zyklon B. Ordinarily used as an insecticide to fumigate barracks and disinfect clothing, it consisted of crystals of prussic acid, a solid chemical that turns into highly lethal hydrogen cyanide gas when it comes into contact with air. The pellets unleashed their bitter, almondlike odor, and the Russians died within minutes, as did hundreds of other Soviet prisoners of war and ill Polish inmates who were subjected to further experiments. "Protected by a gas mask," Höss wrote later, "I watched the killing myself. In the crowded cells, death came the moment the Zyklon B was thrown in. A short, almost smothered cry, and it was all over."

Zyklon B killed in half the time required by carbon monoxide, and Höss recalled that he was "considerably excited by the efficiency of the experiment." The discovery of the effectiveness of Zyklon B against humans must have struck him as particularly appropriate. For years, his boss Himmler and the other top Nazis had inveighed against the Jews as nothing more than vermin. Now an insecticide would prove to be an instrument of their extermination. It "set my mind to rest," wrote Höss. "Now we had the gas, and we had established a procedure."

Auschwitz came to differ from the death camps of Operation Reinhard in ways other than its particular technology of killing. It grew rapidly into the largest of the German concentration and extermination camps, comprising three main compounds and three dozen satellite camps sprawling over nearly twenty square miles, and housing a peak population of close to 160,000 inmates. Trainloads of Jews were brought here not just from Poland but from virtually every country allied with or occupied by Germany. Along with Gypsies, Jehovah's Witnesses, Poles, and Soviet prisoners of war, the Jews at Auschwitz mined coal, made synthetic rubber and gasoline, and labored in other vital war industries. They endured conditions so horrible and alien that inmates spoke of Auschwitz as "another planet," and an SS physician named Heinz Thilo described it as *anus mundi*—the anus of the world. The great majority of these workers died within a few months and their bodies were disposed of in the up-to-date crematoriums Höss constructed to go with his gas chambers. SS officers liked to taunt inmates who dreamed of escape by telling them: "The only exit is up the chimney."

As at the Reinhard camps, death, not synthetic rubber or munitions, was Auschwitz's primary product. Auschwitz simply operated longer and killed more people. Through the technology of Zyklon B, through execution by firearms and by hanging, through torture, overwork, starvation, and disease, at least one million Jews and a quarter of a million others died there.

Höss began the mass killing of Jews with Zyklon B in the spring of 1942,

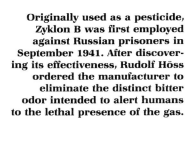

Originally used as a pesticide, Zyklon B was first employed against Russian prisoners in September 1941. After discovering its effectiveness, Rudolf Höss ordered the manufacturer to eliminate the distinct bitter odor intended to alert humans to the lethal presence of the gas.

The workers at Auschwitz were issued striped clothing, such as this tattered jacket worn by one of the inmates. Garments in good repair were prized; according to a survivor, inmates would strip the "still warm body" of a fallen fellow prisoner to get wooden clogs or a coat.

having completed his experimental program on Russians and Poles during the previous months in the converted mortuary of an existing crematorium. The first killing at Auschwitz related to the final solution took place there on May 4 when some 1,200 Jews chosen from recent transports from Germany, Slovakia, and France were gassed.

It was not long before Höss decided that the first killing site was too exposed to the eyes of concentration-camp inmates. He shifted activities to a new, more secluded camp he created about two miles west of the main installation at Auschwitz. This camp was built around two old peasant cottages, charmingly whitewashed and topped with thatched roofs, that stood in the seclusion of a thick forest. The Germans blocked up most of the windows and added airtight interior walls and doors, subdividing each of the cottages—bunkers no. 1 and no. 2 in camp terminology—into four gas chambers. The new killing center became known as Birkenau because the lovely trees shielding it were birches. It was still part of Auschwitz, however, and history would know it by that less euphonious name.

Höss and his SS staff honed their killing techniques, developing new procedures as they learned from their mistakes. He became a fierce professional rival of Operation Reinhard's chief executioner, Christian Wirth, who remained a stubborn proponent of carbon monoxide despite the demonstrated advantages of Zyklon B. The two men refused to share ideas.

One thing Höss learned the hard way was to have his victims disrobe before they were lured into the gas chambers. The first deportees were gassed fully dressed, and their clothing became so stained with feces, urine, and menstrual blood that none of it could be reclaimed for later use. Subsequent deportees were forced to undress in the open air before entering the gas chambers. When Höss noted that this caused them embarrassment and apprehension, he designated nearby barracks where men and women could disrobe in some privacy. "It was most important," he wrote later, "that the whole business of arriving and undressing should take place in an atmosphere of greatest possible calm." To this end, he formed a string orchestra of female inmates, dressed them in white blouses and dark blue skirts, and had them play cheerful pieces as the trainloads of deportees arrived at Auschwitz station, from which they marched or were trucked to Birkenau.

Despite these improvements, it became clear during Birkenau's first months of operation that the physical facilities were inadequate for killing on a massive scale. Himmler visited the camp that summer and gave Höss his approval for an ambitious expansion scheme. Crews of inmates began building a complex of four state-of-the-art killing centers. Each was a brick crematorium containing under one roof all the necessary facilities for the complete extermination process, from undressing through gassing to cremation in specially designed furnaces.

The first of the crematoriums began operations in March 1943. Prominent guests came from Berlin to witness the special inaugural program: the gassing and cremation of Jews from Krakow. The additional crematoriums were completed during the following three months. The four killing centers together contained a total of six gas chambers and fourteen ovens for cremating up to 8,000 corpses a day. Yet, with their steep roofs, dormer windows, stout chimneys, and tasteful landscaping, these one-story red brick structures resembled, at first glance, modern German industrial buildings—large bakeries, perhaps.

Birkenau's crematoriums brought mass murder to new heights of efficiency. In the two largest complexes, the victims descended a flight of steps into underground facilities. The SS executioners herded them into large anterooms with promises of a bath, persuaded them to undress and to hang their clothing neatly on numbered hooks, and then pushed them into a chamber, the largest of which was more than 250 square yards in area.

The Auschwitz orchestra performs for inmates. The musicians played cheerful tunes, such as Chopin's "Barcarolle," and selections from Franz Lehár's *The Merry Widow* to quell the fears of the prisoners as they debarked from the trains.

The chamber contained, in addition to fake water taps and shower nozzles, a row of concrete pillars and, interspersed among them, several hollow floor-to-ceiling columns with perforated metal sides.

As soon as the heavy steel door was bolted shut, an ambulance with phony Red Cross markings pulled up outside the crematoriums. The so-called disinfectors—SS men wearing gas masks and carrying green tin canisters of Zyklon B—jumped out and strode onto the grassy terrace that covered the chamber. They lifted steel trapdoors concealed by mushroomlike concrete forms projecting above the terrace and knocked open the canisters. The necessary amount of Zyklon B had been carefully calculated beforehand; researchers had determined that exterminating human beings required a dose of one milligram per kilogram of body weight.

Upon command—"All right, give them something nice to chew on," was the cruel signal shouted by Sergeant Major Otto Moll—the disinfectors poured the pea-size pellets through the duct into the perforated columns. Then, the motors on the trucks that had carried the victims from the railroad station were revved up to drown out the "heartrending weeping, cries for help, fervent prayers, violent banging, and knocking," according to Filip Müller, who served for two and a half years on the *Sonderkommando*, the special squad of inmates charged with body disposal.

The Zyklon B crystals rattled to the bottom of the columns and sublimed into hydrogen cyanide gas. The very young and the very old died before the others because the gas saturated the lower part of the room first. The stronger ones struggled upward to the better air, trying to gain an extra minute or two of life by clawing and trampling on one another, climbing over layers of bodies. But within a few minutes, the deadly gas seeping from the holes filled the chamber, suffocating even the tallest and the strongest. "The time required for the gas to have effect varied according to the weather," explained Höss, "and depended on whether it was damp or dry, cold or warm. It also depended on the quality of the gas, which was never exactly the same, and on the composition of the transports, which might contain a high proportion of healthy Jews, or old and sick, or children."

"After twenty minutes at the latest," Höss went on, "no movement could be discerned." Watching through a peephole in the door for the struggle to end, the SS physician on duty gave the signal to switch on the ventilators that pumped the gas from the room, whereupon it would dissipate harmlessly into the open air. Pockets of gas lingered amid the entangled layers of victims, however, and members of the Sonderkommando wore protective masks when they entered to hose down the dead and clear the chamber. The Sonderkommando pried apart the intertwined corpses, removed gold teeth, and cut the women's hair. Then, using a leather strap looped around a body's wrist, they dragged the dead one at a time onto the elevator, which carried them up one story to the furnace room.

The furnace room roared like an inferno. "The force and heat of the flames were so great that the whole room rumbled and trembled," Filip Müller recalled. There were as many as five ovens per chamber, most of which had three compartments each. Below the fire-clay grate in each oven blazed a coke-fed fire kept burning with the aid of electric fans. Pairs of inmates heaped two or three bodies onto a metal stretcher and lifted it onto rollers at the opening of a chamber. They pushed the stretcher in, held the corpses on the grate with a large metal fork, and pulled the stretcher out. Three bodies were consumed in about twenty minutes. Later, inmates with metal scrapers raked out the gray-white ashes from the bottom of the oven. These last remains were trucked to one of the nearby rivers, the Vistula or Sola, and dumped into the water.

To make the burning process more efficient and to save coke, a series of macabre experiments were conducted in one of the Auschwitz crematoriums during the autumn of 1943. Technicians from Topf and Sons, the German firm that had manufactured and installed the furnaces, measured the combustibility of different types of coke and corpses. They concluded that the best oven load consisted of one well-nourished, fast-burning adult, one child, and one emaciated adult already reduced to skin and bones by camp labor. This combination of bodies, once it caught fire, would continue to burn without requiring further amounts of precious coke.

A labor brigade lays a concrete ceiling over a new underground gas chamber at Birkenau during the winter of 1942-1943. A crematorium was then constructed on top; an elevator lifted the bodies from the gas chamber to the furnaces above.

In a photo taken by an SS man, prisoners clear out a crematorium at Birkenau. Corpses arrived at the ovens in rail carts. An oven peephole, whose hinged cover was stamped with the name of furnace manufacturer Topf *(inset)*, afforded inspection of the incinerating bodies.

With the occasional exception of an overheated furnace or some other technical problem, Höss's system worked well. Trainload after trainload of Jews from France, Holland, Germany, and other countries arrived, and the occupants were reduced to ashes in a matter of hours. Major breakdowns in the efficiency of the killing operations were so rare that they instantly entered into the realm of legend and myth.

One such interruption occurred on October 23, 1943, with the arrival of some 1,700 Polish Jews from the Bergen-Belsen concentration camp in Germany. These people had already been victimized repeatedly by Nazi deceptions. Many of them held visas for South American countries, and they had been lured out of hiding in Warsaw during the ghetto uprising the previous spring by Gestapo promises to allow them to emigrate. They then paid large bribes to obtain exit permits. After being shuttled off to Bergen-Belsen, they were deported to Auschwitz under the ruse that they were being taken to Switzerland and to freedom.

Descriptions of what happened when they were herded inside the killing complex at Birkenau differ. But according to Filip Müller, more than half of the Jews had already been pushed into the gas chamber when the remainder, still in the changing room, grew suspicious and refused to undress. SS men became nervous and moved in with sticks flailing.

Suddenly, just as the deportees began to submit, Müller wrote, two SS men "stopped in their tracks, attracted by a strikingly handsome woman with blue-black hair who was taking off her right shoe. The woman, as soon as she noticed that the two men were ogling her, launched into what appeared to be a titillating and seductive striptease act. She had taken off her blouse and was standing in front of her lecherous audience in her brassiere. Then she steadied herself against a concrete pillar with her left arm and bent down, slightly lifting her foot, in order to take off her shoe."

As the SS men stood in rapt fascination, the woman slammed the high heel of her shoe against the forehead of one of them. While he winced in pain, she grabbed his pistol and shot the other German, SS Sergeant Major Josef Schillinger. A sadist roundly hated at Auschwitz for his habit of choking inmates to death while they ate their meager meals, Schillinger slumped to the floor mortally wounded. In the confusion that erupted, the woman wounded another SS man in the leg. Other women clawed at the Germans with their bare hands. The place was plunged into darkness, and the Germans fled in panic.

Soon, Höss arrived to set matters right. He surrounded the complex with a detachment of steel-helmeted SS men armed with spotlights, machine guns, and grenades. Deportees already in the gas chamber were executed in the normal manner; the rest were gunned down. Among them was the brave woman, identified only as a former dancer from Warsaw named Horowitz, who had so dramatically disrupted Birkenau's efficient murder factory. It was the only recorded instance in which an individual effectively turned the tables on the Nazi executioners in the shadow of a gas chamber.

Some of the arrivals at Auschwitz were granted a stay of execution. The selection of incoming deportees was conducted at the railroad siding by one of the camp's score of SS physicians. The doctor would look over the arrivals and classify about one-fourth of them as fit for work—mostly men,

On an inspection tour of Auschwitz in July 1942, Heinrich Himmler saunters through the camp's industrial complex with commandant Rudolf Höss and Max Faust, chief engineer for the I. G. Farben company. Later that day, poring over plans to expand the facility, the weary SS chief wipes perspiration from his brow *(right)*.

but also healthy-looking young women. A jerk of his thumb signified life or death: to the left, the gas chambers; to the right, a tattooed identification number on the left forearm, shaven skull, striped uniform, and heavy labor.

In addition to the everyday needs of the camp and crematoriums, the SS required labor for such profit-making enterprises as its cement factory, gravel works, and wood-products plant. Most labor intensive of all were the German private industries springing up in Auschwitz and its satellite camps that employed tens of thousands of Jewish inmates along with lesser numbers of Polish, Soviet, French, and British prisoners of war. Krupp, the steel and armaments giant, produced detonator fuses for artillery shells; Siemens, the big electrical manufacturer, turned out intricate parts for aircraft and submarines.

By far the largest industry at Auschwitz was the sprawling synthetic fuel and rubber complex established by I. G. Farben, the petrochemical combine. The plant, constructed and operated in large part by Jewish slave labor, produced fuel and the ersatz rubber known as Buna from the coal that other inmates mined in the outlying camps of Auschwitz. Situated at Monowitz, a few miles east of Auschwitz proper, the prisoners' compound associated with the plant grew so big that by the autumn of 1943 it was designated as Auschwitz III. The old main camp, now in the geographical center, became Auschwitz I, and Birkenau, farther west, was Auschwitz II.

I. G. Farben and the other private enterprises at Auschwitz paid the SS up to six reichsmarks per day for every skilled worker— $1.50—and the camp devoted less than a dime of that to keeping a laborer alive. Workers got watery soup for lunch and an ounce of bread bulked up by sawdust with perhaps a little margarine for supper; they endured the most primitive sanitary facilities and received practically no medicines despite epidemics of typhus and other diseases that ravaged the camps. They marched out to work early in the morning to

music from one of the inmate bands and came back at night carrying their comrades who had collapsed of hunger, overwork, or beatings by the cruel Kapos and other overseers, many of whom the SS had recruited from the ranks of German professional criminals.

To Höss and his SS henchmen, labor was only an intermediate step en route to death. At periodic selections, workers were forced to parade naked before an SS doctor whose thumb sent to the gas chambers anyone deemed no longer fit for labor. The first to go were the so-called Mussulmans—prisoners reduced to a zombielike state by physical and spiritual exhaustion and so named because the Germans thought they resembled Moslems at their prayers. Men who began the work regime in good health typically survived for only about three months before they, too, in the cruel argot of the SS, "went up the chimney," and were replaced by fresh arrivals.

In addition to selecting workers from the arriving trains, the SS physicians also chose deportees to serve as human guinea pigs for medical experiments. Dr. Edmund König, for example, investigated the effects of electric shock on the brains of Jewish teenagers. Dr. Heinz Thilo performed appendectomies and other surgery on subjects without any symptoms simply to perfect his technique. Research papers detailing the experiments, which inflicted pain, maiming, or death on thousands of prisoners, were duly presented at professional medical meetings back in Germany.

One physician, Dr. Wilhelm Hans Münch, a bacteriologist, distinguished himself from a score of colleagues by trying to help prisoners. He obtained medicines and supplies and secretly treated sick inmates at the risk of his own life. "One could react like a normal human being in Auschwitz only for the first few hours," he said later. "Once one had spent some time there, it was impossible to react normally. In that setup, everyone was sullied."

Himmler took a personal interest in the medical research at Auschwitz. He was especially eager to find methods of mass sterilization—presumably as an alternative to direct killing—and he dispatched Dr. Carl Clauberg, a leading German gynecologist, to direct a research program at the camp in 1942. While Clauberg injected various chemicals into the ovaries of Jewish women, other researchers at Auschwitz pursued alternative procedures. Dr. Horst Schumann subjected both men and women to massive doses of radiation; the chief camp physician, Dr. Edward Wirths, experimented with surgical techniques. They learned nothing new, while in some cases causing their subjects pain, severe radiation burns, premature aging, and death. "I had the feeling," recalled Dr. Dora Klein, a Jewish prisoner and physician who was forced to serve as a nurse in Clauberg's clinic, "that I was in a place that was half hell and half lunatic asylum."

The most strikingly memorable of the physicians and medical research-

An aerial photograph taken by the Allies on June 26, 1944, from some 23,500 feet shows the detailed plan of Auschwitz I, II, and III as well as the I. G. Farben plant. Photo interpreters at the time pinpointed the industrial facilities but did not recognize the gas chambers and crematoriums, which were identified after the camp was liberated.

BIRKENAU
(AUSCHWITZ II)

SS BARRACKS

BODY ASHES THROWN
INTO MARSHES

AUSCHWITZ I

SOLA RIVER

VISTULA RIVER

SS WAR INDUSTRIES
(I.G. FARBEN ETC.)

AUSCHWITZ III (BUNA)

ers at Auschwitz was Dr. Josef Mengele. A handsome Bavarian who had a doctorate in philosophy as well as a medical degree, Mengele was thirty-two years old when he arrived at the camp in the spring of 1943 after recuperating from wounds suffered on the eastern front. He loved music, studied Dante, frequently exuded a disarming charm, and was almost always elegantly turned out in a fresh uniform—"smelling of a fine soap or eau de cologne," remembered a woman survivor of Auschwitz.

Unlike many of the SS physicians, who so dreaded selections that they drank heavily beforehand, Mengele relished the process. On the prowl for subjects for his experiments and delighting in demonstrating his life-and-death power, he signaled people to the gas chamber while whistling operatic arias from Wagner. Once, he took aside a group of some 100 rabbis from an arriving transport, ordered them to form a large circle and dance for his amusement, then sent them to the gas chamber.

Mengele saved his most bizarre selection for Yom Kippur, October 1943, the Jewish Day of Atonement. Some 2,000 boys were gathered on a soccer field when he roared up on his motorcycle. Mengele had a guard nail a plank on one of the goalposts and ordered the boys to walk under the board. The boys understood instantly: Anyone who did not measure to the marker would be selected for death. "It was 100 percent clear to everyone what the purpose of this game was," recalled Josef Kleinman, who was fourteen years old and too short. "We all began stretching. Everyone wanted to get another half-inch, another centimeter."

Young Kleinman desperately stuffed stones and rags in his shoes to add height. When he realized he was still too short, he managed to hide among some taller youths and elude the test. Half of the boys failed to reach Mengele's capricious standard, and they were taken away to be gassed. Kleinman later pointed out that Mengele was literally playing God: The German knew of the Jewish prayer, traditionally recited on Yom Kippur, that tells of the flock being led beneath the rod of the shepherd—the Lord—who then decides which of them will live.

Mengele had volunteered for Auschwitz for the opportunity to pursue research. He had worked at the Nazi-sponsored Institute for Heredity and Eugenics in Frankfurt before the war and wanted to investigate one of Himmler's favorite topics: the biology of racial differences. At Auschwitz, he selected for study about 1,500 sets of identical and fraternal twins, most of them Jewish children, who received extra food, a bit of candy, and a temporary reprieve from death for participating in his research. "Savior and demon," one twin who survived said of Mengele.

Using one twin for the control, Mengele would experiment with the other, carefully writing the data down in Latin and in German. He took blood, injected chemicals, exposed the subject to radiation, performed experimental surgery, and frequently ordered one or both twins killed so he could study them at autopsy. Perhaps because he envisioned an improved, blue-eyed Aryan race, eye pigmentation intrigued him. Vera Kriegel, one of the experimental twins, later described her shock when she saw, at the age of five, the specimens displayed on Mengele's laboratory wall— scores of human eyes "pinned like butterflies." Vera and her sister Olga were among the fewer than 200 twins who survived the research and Auschwitz. Mengele also spared their mother, Vera recalled, because he "wanted to know why our eyes were brown while our mother's were blue."

Other physical anomalies also fascinated Mengele. In an attempt to demonstrate the purported genetic degeneracy of Jews, he selected people with physical deformities, ordered them executed, and then had their flesh boiled away so that the skeletons could be studied. Among the Gypsies, he discovered a family of ten that included seven dwarfs, whom he subjected to painful experimentation, and then forced to perform nude before an audience of SS men. They became part of what one prisoner described as Mengele's "private zoo." "He did whatever pleased him," said Olga Lengyel, an inmate-doctor. "He was not a savant. His was the mania of a collector."

The Gypsies whom Mengele collected for his experiments lived in the Gypsy camp, thirty barracks of Block B2 at Birkenau. The camp had been established in February 1943, when the Germans began deporting Gypsies from Germany and other parts of Europe to Auschwitz. The Gypsy camp soon reached its 10,000-person capacity, and for the eighteen months of its existence, these deportees were treated differently from the Jews. They could live together as families, and few were put to work outside their own compound. There was even a playground where the Gypsy children were sometimes made to pose for German photographers. For propaganda reasons, or because of the medical experiments, the Gypsies were spared. Then Berlin sent new orders. In 1944, thousands of able-bodied Gypsy prisoners were shipped off to slave labor in other concentration camps. The remaining Gypsies at Auschwitz—about 3,000—went to the gas chambers, becoming part of the more than 250,000 Gypsies who died at the hands of the Germans during the war.

In addition to the Gypsy compound, the Germans maintained another unusual camp in the Birkenau section of Auschwitz. The family camp in Block B2 originally consisted of about 5,000 Czech Jews; like the Gypsies, these inmates remained together in their families, had their own orchestra, and were spared forced labor. The first of them arrived in September 1943 from Theresienstadt near Prague, a place that the Nazis referred to as a

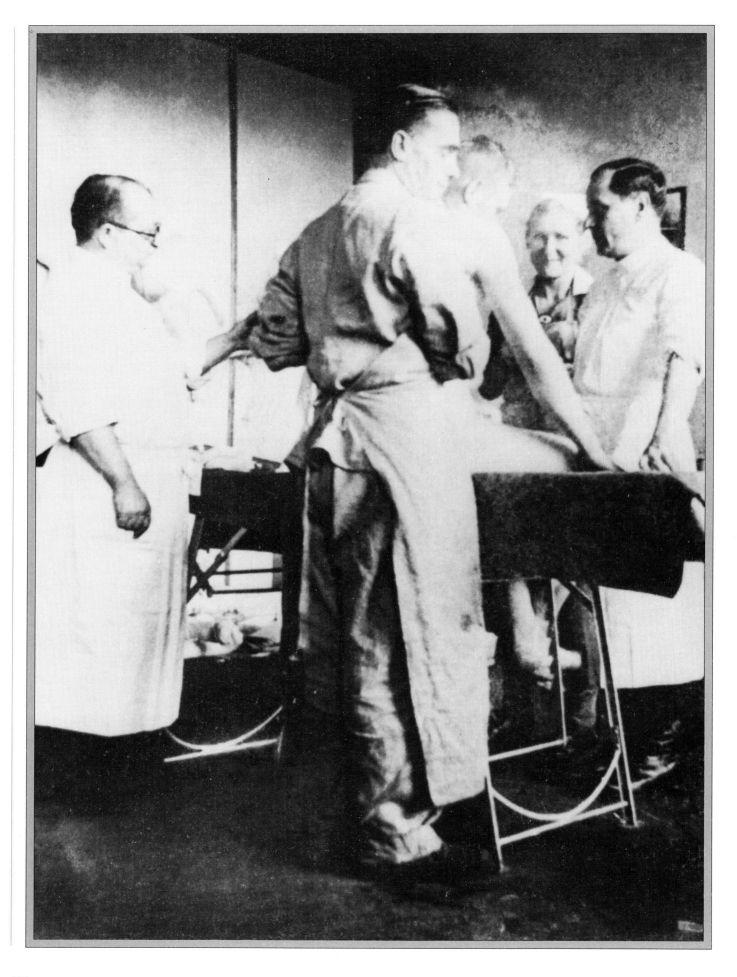

model ghetto, but which was in fact just a dressed-up version of a transit and concentration camp.

Himmler had established this ghetto in 1942 by emptying the old fortress town of Theresienstadt of its inhabitants and filling it with more than 50,000 Jews. They were a mixture of prominent artists and leaders, disabled or decorated veterans of World War I, and the elderly, mostly from the Czech provinces of Bohemia and Moravia. In Theresienstadt, Himmler wanted to create a kind of showcase ghetto to counter stories about the evils of his concentration camps. The SS even made a propaganda film of the place, intending to demonstrate that the Jews were well treated and contented. In fact, perhaps 30,000 people died there of exposure, disease, and starvation, and more than twice that number were transported eastward to the death camps.

Although most deportees from Theresienstadt were gassed immediately upon arrival at Auschwitz, a few were diverted to the family camp further to serve Himmler's grand deception. To heighten the illusion that Auschwitz was a benign concentration camp and not a killing center, representatives of the International Red Cross were allowed to visit the family camp. Occupants were permitted to receive parcels from home and encouraged to write postcards to friends and relatives. Family-camp residents typically survived for a period of six months. Then, like almost all the others at Auschwitz who had been spared immediate death, their reprieve came to an end in the nearby killing facilities at Birkenau.

Himmler's program of deception proved so successful that Birkenau was one of the best-kept secrets of the war. It went undetected until the summer of 1944, despite the fact that word of the mass killings had leaked out on several occasions.

The sadistic Dr. Josef Mengele cut such a dashing figure that some female inmates actually admired him. One prisoner called him a "beautiful person" while others described him as "gorgeous" and even "kindly."

Dr. Carl Clauberg (far left) and his staff operate on an inmate. He told women victims that they were being artificially inseminated; instead, he injected a chemical into their ovaries that caused sterilization and severe pain.

In 1942, Lieutenant Kurt Gerstein, the Berlin-based SS officer responsible for procuring Zyklon B, had revealed everything to a Swedish diplomat. Gerstein, a trained engineer, had been dispatched that summer to the Reinhard death camps, where he witnessed the killing procedures.

Heading home on the Warsaw-Berlin express, Gerstein encountered a Swedish diplomat named Baron von Otter. Gerstein was sweating profusely, obviously upset, and the Swede offered him a cigarette to calm his nerves. "May I tell you a grim story?" asked Gerstein. He went on to describe what he had witnessed at Belzec, Treblinka, and Sobibor, and presumably to mention the purpose of the poisonous gas he supplied to Auschwitz. Von Otter sent Stockholm a detailed report of his startling conversation

with Gerstein, but the Swedish government, eager to avoid tension with Germany, did not disclose the information.

In any case, definitive word about the Reinhard camps soon reached Britain and the United States. Late in 1942, Jan Karski, an intrepid courier from the Polish underground who had gained firsthand knowledge of the camps, arrived in London with a detailed report. The Allies were in no military position to take action against the camps; they could do little but issue stern warnings against the "bestial crimes." But even after the Reinhard camps ceased operations, Auschwitz remained shrouded in secrecy; it was the "unknown destination" referred to in many reports of deportations from western Europe. Isolated references to it failed to make an impression in London and Washington. In fact, on April 4, 1944, an American reconnaissance plane actually flew over Auschwitz and photographed the I. G. Farben synthetic rubber factory at Monowitz. The Buna plant and portions of the Auschwitz main camp showed up clearly, but the gas chambers at Birkenau were not recognized for what they were.

By then, more than 500,000 Jews had been gassed at Auschwitz, and the worst was yet to come. During that April, the camp began feverish preparations to receive transports from Hungary, the last German-occupied country to deport its Jews. Slave-labor gangs worked around the clock to get ready for that country's estimated 750,000 Jews, whom the SS men cynically referred to as "Hungarian salami." The laborers gave a fresh coat of paint to the gas chambers, overhauled the crematoriums, dug five extra cremation pits to handle the anticipated overflow of corpses, and refurbished one of the two old Birkenau farmhouses originally used for gassing. They also rushed to complete a new three-track rail spur enabling the trains to roll on through the Auschwitz station and carry victims directly to the Birkenau killing complexes.

Höss also made a key personnel change to ensure smooth operations. He appointed as overseer of all the crematoriums Sergeant Major Otto Moll, who had supervised the burning of the exhumed corpses in the summer of 1942. A short, thickset man with freckles and a glass eye, Moll wore a

An Auschwitz inmate is labeled with an identification number and the letter Z, for Zigeuner, or Gypsy. Although Gypsies were initially allowed to live together with their families, many of them died of starvation and disease in their camp at Birkenau.

Four malnourished Gypsy children, subjects of Dr. Mengele's experiments, stand naked under the cold scrutiny of an SS camera at Auschwitz. One of Mengele's special interests was the effect of starvation on infants and children.

white uniform and liked to boast that he would burn his own wife and seven-year-old child if so ordered by the Führer. Possessed of a "morbid partiality for obscene and salacious tortures," as Müller later wrote of him, Moll was fond of such practices as hurling live babies into the burning pits and using naked young women for target practice.

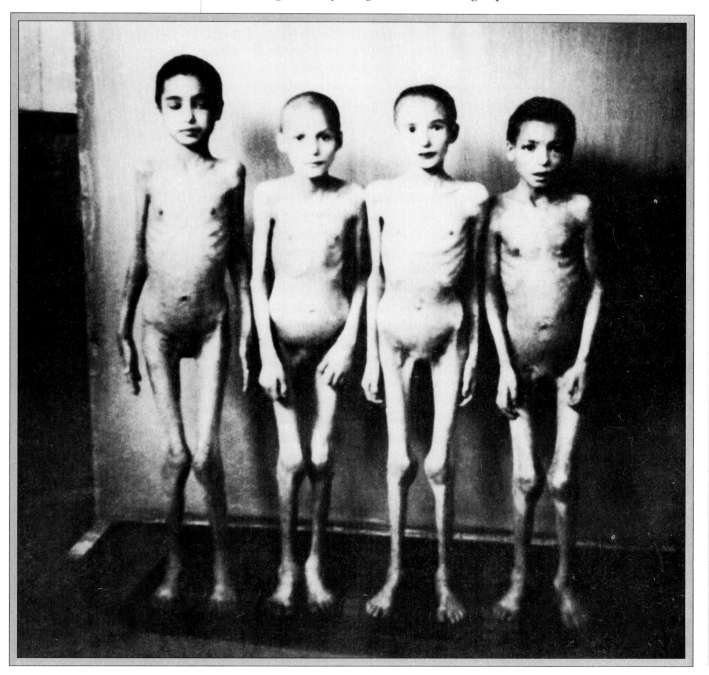

Höss knew Moll to be a ruthlessly efficient organizer, just the sort he needed to speed disposal of the expected deluge of Hungarian Jews. Moll gave no sign of disappointing these expectations: In the new cremation pits, he soon had laborers digging out drainage channels that were sloped so that the fat from the burning bodies would run down and collect in pans. The fat could then be poured back on the fire to make it burn faster.

Hitler opened the way for the deportation of the Hungarian Jews during the spring of 1944 by clamping down on his Hungarian allies. The Hungarians were opportunists who had joined the Axis early in the war partly in order to annex neighboring territory. Hitler found them to be unenthusiastic partners and was especially miffed at what he regarded as their "irresolute and ineffective" handling of the Jewish question. To be sure, Hungary had discriminatory laws in place, and the septuagenarian chief of state, Admiral Miklós Horthy de Nagybánya, was a self-proclaimed, lifelong anti-Semite. But Horthy had repeatedly refused to deport his nation's Jews, the largest such community surviving in German-dominated Europe. By 1944, he was secretly hoping to make a separate peace with the Allies and was loath to undermine that possibility by disturbing the Jews, who were highly visible, forming the backbone of professional and commercial life in Hungary. Hitler had other plans. To forestall the possibility of a Hungarian capitulation, and to protect his southern flank, Hitler sent troops into Hungary on March 19, forcing Horthy to appoint a new and more compliant government.

Adolf Eichmann and his staff arrived in Budapest on the heels of the German troops. Assured of Hungarian cooperation, he established headquarters in the Majestic Hotel and started work with the sure touch he had acquired in nearly three years of shipping people to concentration and extermination camps from all over Europe. He gathered top Jewish leaders, told them, "I am a bloodhound," and ordered them to establish a Jewish council to carry out German dictates. Then, with the help of Hungarian police, he began concentrating Hungary's Jews in makeshift ghettos and improvised camps in six carefully delineated deportation zones.

Mass deportations began on May 15. Several times a day for weeks on end, at a time when the German armies needed every man and gun that could be mustered to stave off the advance of the Red Army, train after train was diverted to Hungary. The transports typically consisted of more than forty sealed freight cars. As many as 100 Jews were crammed into each car with one bucket of drinking water and one waste bucket for a journey of approximately 200 miles, which sometimes required four days. At Auschwitz, the trains rolled onto the newly completed spur and right up to the Birkenau crematoriums. On May 21, the new sidings there were backed up almost to Auschwitz station with no fewer than six trains from Hungary, Holland, and Belgium.

Only a handful of deportees from these early Hungarian transports were spared the gas chambers and sent to the labor gangs. Elie Wiesel, the eloquent chronicler of the Holocaust who was then fourteen years old, was one of the lucky few, selected along with his father to work at the I. G. Farben rubber factory. But he wrote later that as they stood in line after the selection, no one knew for sure which of the two lines led to work and which to death. "Around us," he recalled, "everyone was weeping. Someone began to recite the *Kaddish*, the Hebrew prayer for the dead. I do not know if it has ever happened before, in the long history of the Jews, that people have ever recited the prayer for the dead for themselves."

Many of the early arrivals at Auschwitz were handed postcards after they entered the disrobing rooms. SS men ordered them to write home that they had arrived at "Waldsee," a mythical camp where they had found work and lacked for nothing. These messages had the desired effect back in Hungary. Moshe Sandberg, whose family in the town of Kecskemet received such a card from his father, later wrote: "The postcards acted as a sleeping drug, coming just at the right time to tranquilize us, to dispel the accumulated misgivings of the past weeks, and to remove any thought of revolt or escape."

Never had the killing complexes been called upon to operate at such a pace. In only twenty-three days, the Germans counted precisely 289,357 Hungarian Jews deported; most of them died. Up to 12,000 persons a day entered the chambers at Birkenau. To dispose of their remains, the crematorium crews of the Sonderkommando were quadrupled to nearly 900 laborers. Smoke from the chimneys and open burning pits blotted out the sun and blanketed the moon. Mountains of ashes piled up too rapidly for the trucks to haul them away, and the residue had to be buried in newly dug pits. A crew of Greek Jews stomped the ashes, moving their feet in rhythm with their nonstop singing in order to pulverize any protruding remains.

On June 16, at the very peak of the killing, the Allies at last became aware of what was happening at Auschwitz. Eyewitness reports from two pairs of escaped prisoners reached London and Washington via Geneva from occupied Slovakia. The reports of Rudolf Vrba and Alfred Wetzler, both Slovaks, recounted in detail the gassing procedures at Birkenau; statements by Arnost Rosin, a Slovak, and Czeslaw Mordowicz, a Pole, described the

Jewish orderlies assigned to oversee transport columns from the Theresienstadt ghetto to the Czech family camp at Auschwitz wore armbands like the one pictured above, in addition to their yellow stars.

arrival and the killing of the Hungarian Jews. The shocking news, combined with the earlier eyewitness accounts of the other extermination camps, moved Prime Minister Winston Churchill of Britain to write an associate, "There is no doubt that this is probably the greatest and most horrible crime ever committed in the whole history of the world."

A storm of protests descended on Hungary's Admiral Horthy. Messages urging him to stop the deportations came from the president of the International Red Cross, the king of Sweden, and the pope. More disturbing to him were intercepted British and American teletype messages that raised the possibility of bombing raids on government offices in Budapest and postwar reprisals against prominent Hungarian officials. Finally, Horthy acted. On July 9, after more than half of Hungary's Jews—437,402 by German count—had been sent away, he ordered the deportations halted.

International Jewish leaders, meanwhile, urged the British and Americans to initiate a bombing campaign to disrupt the rail traffic between Hungary and Auschwitz and to destroy the Birkenau killing centers. The Allies refused, although Poland now lay within range of bombers based in newly liberated southern Italy. If the gas chambers were bombed, the Allies pointed out, the Germans would find other means of carrying out the final solution. And, they continued, targeting Birkenau would only divert the Allied air forces from their mission of destroying the strategic industries that sustained the Nazi war machine, thus delaying the final victory that would halt the destruction of the Jews.

Ironically, on August 20, B-17 bombers from the American Fifteenth Air Force actually hit Auschwitz. They delivered the first of four attacks on the I. G. Farben facility at Monowitz, a few miles east of the gas chambers. The storm of bombs stirred joy and hope among the 30,000 Jewish slave laborers at Monowitz even though they were now doubly endangered. "We wanted once to see a killed German," recalled one of them, Arie Hassenberg. "Then we could sleep better. That was why we enjoyed the bombing."

Less than a month later, on September 13, Hassenberg got his wish. Bombs from American B-24s attacking Monowitz fell short and destroyed a barracks at the Auschwitz main camp, killing fifteen SS men and injuring twenty-eight. A cluster of bombs was also mistakenly dropped farther west at Birkenau, damaging the railroad but missing the crematoriums.

The refusal of the Allies to intentionally bomb the rail lines or Birkenau lent added urgency to an unusual rescue mission being mounted in Budapest during the summer and autumn of 1944. The participants included diplomats from five neutral nations—Portugal, Spain, Sweden, Turkey, and Switzerland—along with the papal nuncio and representatives of

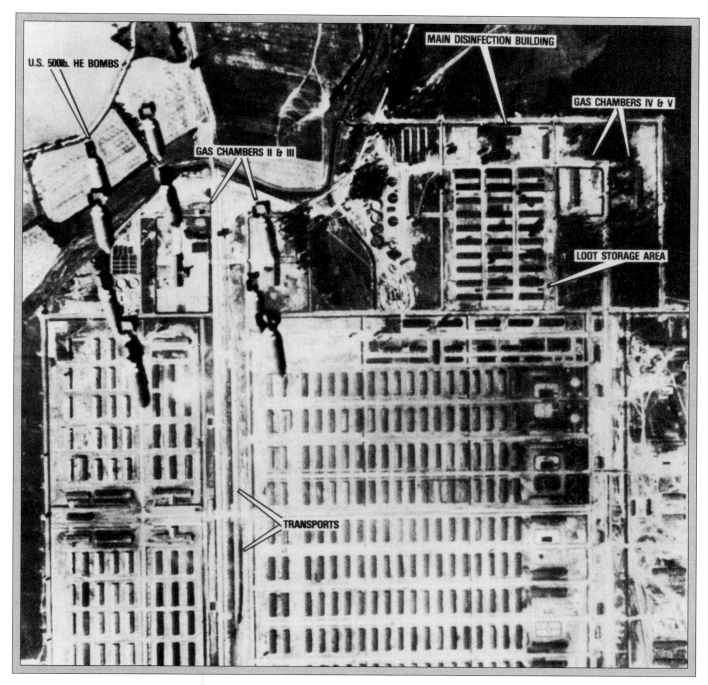

GAS CHAMBERS II & III

MAIN DISINFECTION BUILDING

GAS CHAMBERS IV & V

U.S. 500lb. HE BOMBS

LOOT STORAGE AREA

TRANSPORTS

An aerial photograph taken on September 13, 1944, shows eight misdirected bombs falling on Birkenau, where they damaged the railroads but missed the crematoriums. The Allies intended to hit the nearby I. G. Farben complex, but they were unsure of the function of the buildings at Birkenau.

the International Red Cross. In an effort to protect the nearly 200,000 Jews remaining in Budapest in the event deportations to Auschwitz resumed, they issued thousands of diplomatic letters of protection intended to safeguard the bearers, and then secured the recipients in hundreds of special apartment buildings.

A trio of foreigners, working with the Jewish underground in Budapest, took the lead in this unprecedented mission of mercy. One was Charles Lutz, the Swiss consul, a forty-nine-year-old career diplomat who not only was instrumental in issuing more than 8,000 safe-conduct passes but also assisted the Jewish underground in setting up an operation to print tens of thousands of additional passes. Another angel of mercy was Giorgio Perlasca, an Italian meat importer who himself had sought protection from the Spanish embassy in Budapest after the overthrow of Mussolini made his compatriots suspect in Axis countries. Armed with a diplomatic passport, he helped the Spanish embassy issue letters of protection and set up safe houses for some 5,200 Jews. He continued this work even after the approach of the Soviet army forced the closing of the embassy—by the simple expedient of appointing himself the Spanish chargé d'affaires.

Another figure in the rescue efforts was the young Swede Raoul Wallenberg. The progeny of prominent bankers, diplomats, and industrialists, Wallenberg, aged thirty-two, was a charming and cultivated businessman, an executive in an export-import firm. His ancestral connections to Judaism were slight: His great-great-grandfather was a German Jew who had sought haven in Stockholm from anti-Semitism in his homeland. Wallenberg's nominal role in Budapest was that of attaché of the Swedish legation, but he was there primarily at the instigation of the War Refugee Board, a new United States government agency established to help Jewish victims.

Wallenberg arrived in Budapest on July 9, the day that deportations of the Hungarian Jews to Auschwitz halted. He quickly moved to expand the issuing of safe-conduct passes to Jews, and it was not long before some 10,000 of the Swedish documents were in circulation. Like the papers handed out by the Swiss, Spanish, and other legations, Wallenberg's passes had no real standing or precedent under international law. But Wallenberg proved to be so adept at cajoling and bribing Hungarian officials that the government formally recognized and respected these documents.

The work of Wallenberg and his colleagues built to a fever pitch during the autumn. In mid-October, the Germans engineered the overthrow of Admiral Horthy after he attempted to negotiate a separate peace with the Soviet Union, whose forces already had crossed into Hungary. The SS installed the Hungarian fascist extremists known as the Arrow Cross and brought back Adolf Eichmann to resume deportations. Wallenberg, working day and night with a staff of nearly 400 Hungarian Jews, set up a children's home and soup kitchens. In November, he negotiated for the creation of an "international ghetto" where thousands of Jews were housed under the protection of the neutral legations. He raced down to the rail yards to rescue Jews with Swedish passports from Auschwitz-bound trains; to the consternation of the Germans and Hungarian police, he even climbed on the roof of the cars and handed out passes to those who lacked them. When Eichmann, faced with a shortage of rail cars, began marching tens of thousands of Jews westward to slave labor in Austria, Wallenberg and the Swiss diplomat Charles Lutz drove along the route of march, boldly pulling from the ranks hundreds who carried protective papers.

In Budapest, perhaps 100,000 Jews were now in safe houses maintained by the neutral nations. They and nearly 25,000 other Jews in the city were not immune to the random, vicious attacks by roving bands of Arrow Cross

The Swedish attaché Raoul Wallenberg saved the lives of tens of thousands of Jews in Budapest by issuing protective passports and establishing safe houses. His humanitarian efforts drew the ire of Adolf Eichmann, who threatened, "I shall kill the Jew-dog Wallenberg."

thugs, but they did remain safe from Auschwitz and the death marches until the Russian liberation of Budapest in January 1945. One of their saviors, Wallenberg, met a mysterious end. He was arrested by the Russians on suspicion of espionage and vanished. More than a decade after the war, the Russians reported that he had died in a Soviet prison in 1947.

The suspension of deportations from Hungary to Auschwitz in July 1944 threw the Sonderkommando at the killing camp into a crisis. These crematorium crews knew full well that they were living on borrowed time, that once the trains ceased to arrive, their usefulness—and doubtless their lives—would come to an end. In the best of times, these workers, almost all of whom were Jews, led lives of anguish and despair. To be sure, they were able to supply themselves amply with food, cigarettes, and valuables by confiscating—"organizing," in camp parlance—such things from the belongings of the gas-chamber victims. They were also able to barter for other goods by dealing with workers in the nearby section of Birkenau known as "Canada," where the victims' belongings were sorted and stored before being sent on to the Reich.

At the same time, however, the crematorium crews had to perform such dehumanizing work that some prisoners volunteered for the gas chambers rather than serve. And now death loomed for all. "It stood to reason," wrote Filip Müller, "that the perpetrators of daily mass murders would not allow a single witness of their crimes to stay alive and to testify against them."

Müller and the others had realized that only a mass escape would save them, and during the spring and summer of 1944, while nearly 400,000 Hungarian Jews were being gassed, the Sonderkommando developed elaborate plans for a revolt. Their positions of privilege enabled them to prepare for the uprising. They obtained small arms from workers in the camp shops where downed airplanes were dismantled. They arranged with Jewish female workers at the Union munitions factory to smuggle out explosives in the false bottoms of food trays. Their plans for an uprising that also included destruction of the crematoriums were coordinated with the campwide underground movement, whose leadership was dominated by Polish gentiles. But these camp resistance leaders repeatedly postponed

the scheduled revolt, and as the Red Army advanced from the east—in early September, Soviet forces were less than 100 miles from Auschwitz—they were increasingly inclined to sit tight until the anticipated liberation.

Inside the crematoriums, however, the stresses reached a breaking point in the early autumn. With the transports from Hungary still halted, Sergeant Major Moll and the SS overseers decided to reduce the 863-man Sonderkommando. During the last week in September, they selected 200 members and gassed them. A week or so later, the names of some 300 additional workers—nearly half of the remaining Sonderkommando—were placed on a new selection list, supposedly for transfer to another camp. Those on the list, mainly Greek and Hungarian Jews, decided to strike immediately despite the objections of the camp underground and of their comrades in the crematoriums, who had set the date for a week hence.

The revolt erupted about noon on October 7 in the yard outside Crematorium IV. The SS men were conducting a roll call to cull the prisoners on the selection list when they were pelted with a flurry of stones thrown by the inmates who had been selected. Other workers hidden inside the crematorium set fire to rags soaked in oil and wood alcohol, and soon the building was aflame. Truckloads of steel-helmeted SS guards roared up to surround the yard and began firing. But the wail of the camp siren and the leaping flames alerted the work crews in two other crematoriums. They seized the explosives and weapons previously stashed away and raced to

Sonderkommando members drag corpses onto a pyre at Birkenau. Rudolf Höss explained that crematoriums were much preferred to open-air incineration. "When a strong wind was blowing," he wrote, "the stench of burning flesh was carried for many miles and caused the whole neighborhood to talk about the burning of Jews."

cut through the inner cordon of barbed wire around Birkenau. Few got far; some 450 prisoners died during the uprising—half again as many as the Germans had intended to gas that day. In addition, the Germans later hanged the four female factory workers who had helped furnish the explosives. But three SS men had been killed, one crematorium destroyed, and a legend created of men and women who had staged, Filip Müller wrote, "a unique event in the history of Auschwitz."

Although the trains from Hungary had stopped coming, others continued to arrive, and the killings persisted at the remaining crematoriums. Throughout October, Jews died at the rate of more than 1,000 per day. On October 30, the last transport of Jews arrived from the so-called model ghetto at Theresienstadt; on that day and the next, 1,689 of them went to the gas chambers. Then, on November 2, 1944, more than three years after the first gassing experiments at Auschwitz, an order arrived from Heinrich Himmler: "I forbid any further annihilation of Jews." Upon his further orders, all but one of the crematoriums were dismantled, the burning pits covered up and planted with grass, and the gas pipes and other equipment shipped to concentration camps in Germany. The single remaining crematorium was for the disposal of those who died natural deaths and the gassing of about two hundred surviving members of the Sonderkommando.

The final solution was formally over. Although tens of thousands of Jews and others would go on dying of neglect and brutality, the systematic killing had ended. Why Himmler made this decision is not certain. One possible reason was that the Reich was desperate for labor, even Jewish workers. Evidence suggests, however, that Himmler foresaw the disaster

Before retreating from the advancing Russians, SS troops burned storage sheds containing valuables that were taken from the prisoners *(left)*. They also forced some 58,000 inmates on a death march toward Germany. Those who collapsed on the way, including these victims lying along the Auschwitz rail line *(below)*, were summarily shot.

Children of Auschwitz display their camp tattoos to a Red Army photographer. When the Soviets liberated the camp in January 1945, they found among the survivors about 200 children aged six to fourteen.

that awaited the Third Reich and was desperately trying to save his own skin by compiling a record of what he might have termed "leniency." Indeed, his order to stop the killing contained a further, ingratiating directive instructing that "proper care be given to the weak and the sick."

Less than three months later, on January 17, 1945, the last roll call was conducted at Auschwitz. The Germans counted 67,012 prisoners at the main camp and the satellite camps. This amounted to less than half the peak population of 155,000 tabulated during the previous August. Many had already been sent westward to camps in Germany, and more had died. Now, with the artillery of the approaching Red Army thundering on the horizon, the Germans ordered the evacuation of all but about 6,000 inmates who were too infirm to make the trip by train or on foot.

The 58,000 or so evacuees struggled westward in agony. Even those who were put aboard trains underwent privation. Many hundreds died of starvation or exposure in the unheated cars. Many had to march all the way to Germany in freezing cold. Staggering along in rags, barefoot or on wooden clogs, sustained only by a starvation diet, thousands fell by the wayside and were shot by their SS guards. One march lasted for more than sixteen weeks and claimed the lives of all but 280 of the 3,000 who began it. Yehuda Bakon later spoke of marching with a group of orphaned boys who agreed, "It is good that our parents were killed in the gas chambers. They did not have to undergo all this torture and suffering."

Those left behind at Auschwitz suffered too. Without food, water, or heat, sick and despairing, they died by the hundreds each day. The SS guards disappeared by increments until finally the inmates had the camp to themselves. On January 27, the Russians arrived. It was a "beautiful, sunny winter's day," a survivor wrote in his diary. "At about 3:00 p.m., we heard a noise in the direction of the main gate. We hurried to the scene. It was a Soviet foward patrol—Soviet soldiers in white caps! There was a mad rush to shake them by the hand and shout our gratitude. We were liberated!"

By that time, about 2,800 people remained alive at Auschwitz. The soldiers fed the survivors, tended to the sick, and buried the dead. Thousands upon thousands had died before these at Auschwitz, but this mass burial was the "first dignified funeral" ever held there, an inmate observed.

The Soviets searched the camp and found other pieces of the grim legacy of genocide: In storehouses the SS had failed to burn down were 836,255 women's coats and dresses, 368,820 men's suits, and seven tons of human hair. It was the sort of evidence—emaciated corpses, bits of bone, ashes, clothing—that soon would be uncovered in dozens of other Nazi concentration camps liberated by the advancing Allies. For all his efforts, Himmler had been unable to keep the secret of the final solution. Soon the world would have to confront, but would barely comprehend, the reality of the Holocaust that had claimed the lives of 15 million innocent people. ✚

Skeletal corpses await burial at Auschwitz after the liberation. The Russians found thousands of dead and some 2,800 gravely ill survivors, many of whom died within days of gaining their freedom after having endured years of torture and captivity.

Russian soldiers and Polish civilians accompany a mass burial procession that took place shortly after the camp was liberated.

Acknowledgments

The editors thank: France: Paris—Sarah Mimoun, Archiviste, Centre de Documentation Juive Contemporaine. Germany: Berlin—Ruth Gross, Bildarchiv Pisarek; Heidi Klein, Bildarchiv Preussischer Kulturbesitz; Wolfgang Streubel, Ullstein Bilderdienst.

Bonn—Dorothea Seipel, Stadtarchiv. Cologne—Barbara Becker-Jäkli. Frankfurt—Maria Caspers, Historisches Museum; Ernst Klee; Michael Lennarz, Jüdisches Museum. Koblenz—Meinrad Nilges, Bundesarchiv. Seevetal—Günther Schwarberg. Israel:

Jerusalem—Zvi Reiter; Yad Vashem. Kibbutz Lohamei Haghetaot—Avi Hurwitz, Ghetto Fighters' House. United States: District of Columbia—Raye Farr, Charlotte Hebebrand, Genya Markon, Susan Morganstein, United States Holocaust Memorial Museum.

Picture Credits

Credits from left to right are separated by semicolons, from top to bottom by dashes. Cover: Edimedia, Paris. 4, 5: Bildarchiv Preussischer Kulturbesitz, Berlin. 6, 7: Fanny Auerbach, from the collection Juden in Köln by Dieter Corbach, Cologne. 8, 9: Roman Vishniac. 10: Bildarchiv Preussischer Kulturbesitz, Berlin, foto Heinrich Hoffmann. 13: Historisches Museum Frankfurt am Main. 15: Jüdisches Museum Frankfurt Sammlung Bernhard Brilling. 17: Archiv für Kunst und Geschichte, Berlin. 19: Popperfoto, London. 20: Bildarchiv Abraham Pisarek, Berlin. 24, 25: The Hulton Picture Company, London. 26: AP/Wide World, New York. 27: Süddeutscher Verlag Bilderdienst, Munich. 29: Courtesy Time Inc. Magazines Picture Collection (2)—Bildarchiv Preussischer Kulturbesitz, Berlin. 31: Bildarchiv Preussischer Kulturbesitz, Berlin, foto Federmeyer, 1938. 33: Map by R. R. Donnelley and Sons Company, Cartographic Services. 34: Photograph by Arnold Kramer, © 1991 United States Holocaust Memorial Museum, Washington, D.C. 35: Jüdisches Museum Frankfurt Sammlung Getto Lodz. 36, 37: Robert Hunt Library, London; Süddeutscher Verlag Bilderdienst, Munich. 38, 39: Stadt Hadamar. 40-47: Bundesarchiv, Koblenz. 48: © Günther Schwarberg, Seevetal—Heinrich Jöst. 49: Heinrich Jöst. 50-57: Heinrich Jöst, © Günther Schwarberg, Seevetal. 58: Süddeutscher Verlag Bilderdienst, Munich. 60, 61: International News Photo/Bettmann, New York. 64, 65: Main Commission for Investigation of Nazi Crimes, Warsaw; Süddeutscher Verlag Bilderdienst, Munich. 67: Süddeutscher Verlag Bilderdienst, Munich. 69:

Central Photo Agency, Warsaw. 70, 71: Photograph by Arnold Kramer, © 1991 United States Holocaust Memorial Museum, Washington, D.C.—Bundesarchiv, Koblenz. 73: Main Commission for Investigation of Nazi Crimes, Warsaw. 75: Archiv Ernst Klee, Frankfurt. 76, 77: Courtesy Yad Vashem, Jerusalem. 78, 79: Heinrich Hoffmann, © Time Inc. 80, 81: J. Schatz, United States Holocaust Memorial Museum, Washington, D.C. 84, 85: Courtesy Yad Vashem, Jerusalem. 86, 87: Bildarchiv Preussischer Kulturbesitz, Berlin. 89-91: Czechoslovak News Agency, Prague. 92, 93: Archiv J. K. Piekalkiewicz Rösrath-Hoffnungsthal. 94, 95: Czechoslovak News Agency, Prague. 96, 97: Bildarchiv Preussischer Kulturbesitz, Berlin; Ullstein Bilderdienst, Berlin. 98: Courtesy Yad Vashem, Jerusalem. 100, 101: Photographs by Arnold Kramer, © 1991 United States Holocaust Memorial Museum, Washington, D.C. 104: Archiv Ernst Klee, Frankfurt. 105: Main Commission for Investigation of Nazi Crimes, Warsaw. 106: Bildarchiv Preussischer Kulturbesitz, Berlin. 107: Main Commission for Investigation of Nazi Crimes, Warsaw. 108, 109: Courtesy Yad Vashem, Jerusalem. 111: Central Photo Agency, Warsaw. 113: Photographs by Hubert Pfoch, Vienna. 116, 117: Bildarchiv Preussischer Kulturbesitz, Berlin. 118, 119: Main Commission for Investigation of Nazi Crimes, Warsaw. 121-123: Archiv Ernst Klee, Frankfurt. 125-127: Beit Lohamei Haghetaot (Photo and Film/The Art Museum/Library), Israel. 130, 131: The Hulton Picture Company, London. 132, 133: Ullstein Bilderdienst, Berlin; Süddeutscher Verlag

Bilderdienst, Munich. 134, 135: Süddeutscher Verlag Bilderdienst, Munich (2)—Central Photo Agency, Warsaw; from *Final Journey: The Fate of the Jews in Nazi Europe,* Mayflower Books, New York, 1979. 136, 137: Central Photo Agency, Warsaw; Keystone, Paris—Main Commission for Investigation of Nazi Crimes, Warsaw. 138, 139: Archiv für Kunst und Geschichte, Berlin—Ullstein Bilderdienst, Berlin. 140-149: Courtesy Yad Vashem, Jerusalem. 150: Courtesy State Museum of Auschwitz/Birkenau. 153: Photographs by Arnold Kramer, © 1991 United States Holocaust Memorial Museum, Washington, D.C. 155-159: Courtesy State Museum of Auschwitz/Birkenau. 160, 161: Main Commission for Investigation of Nazi Crimes, Warsaw—Süddeutscher Verlag Bilderdienst, Munich. 163: National Archives, courtesy United States Holocaust Memorial Museum, Washington, D.C. 166: Secrétariat d'Etat Chargé des Anciens Combattants et des Victimes de Guerre, Mission Permanente aux Commémorations et à l'Information Historique. 167: Süddeutscher Verlag Bilderdienst, Munich. 168: Archives du Centre de Documentation Juive Contemporaine, Paris. 169: Main Commission for Investigation of Nazi Crimes, Warsaw. 171: Photograph by Arnold Kramer, © 1991 United States Holocaust Memorial Museum, Washington, D.C. 173: National Archives, courtesy United States Holocaust Memorial Museum, Washington, D.C. 175: AP/Wide World, New York. 176: Courtesy State Museum of Auschwitz/Birkenau. 177: Süddeutscher Verlag Bilderdienst, Munich. 178-183: Courtesy State Museum of Auschwitz/Birkenau.

Bibliography

Books

Ainsztein, Reuben, *Jewish Resistance in Nazi-Occupied Eastern Europe*. New York: Barnes & Noble, 1974.

Arad, Yitzhak, *Belzec, Sobibor, Treblinka*. Bloomington: Indiana University Press, 1987.

Arad, Yitzhak, ed., *The Pictorial History of the Holocaust*. New York: Macmillan, 1990.

Astor, Gerald, *The "Last" Nazi*. New York: Donald I. Fine, 1985.

Bauer, Yehuda, *A History of the Holocaust*. New York: Franklin Watts, 1982.

Berenbaum, Michael, ed., *A Mosaic of Victims*. New York: New York University Press, 1990.

Bridgman, Jon, *The End of the Holocaust*. Ed. by Richard H. Jones. Portland, Ore.: Areopagitica Press, 1990.

Calic, Edouard, *Reinhard Heydrich*. Transl. by Lowell Bair. New York: Military Heritage Press, 1982.

Chamberlin, Brewster, and Marcia Feldman, eds., *The Liberation of the Nazi Concentration Camps, 1945*. Washington, D.C.: United States Holocaust Memorial Council, 1987.

Dallin, Alexander, *German Rule in Russia*. New York: Octagon Books, 1980.

Dawidowicz, Lucy S., *The War against the Jews, 1933-1945*. New York: Holt, Rinehart and Winston, 1975.

Deschner, Günther, *Reinhard Heydrich*. New York: Stein and Day, 1981.

Donat, Alexander, *The Holocaust Kingdom*. New York: Holocaust Library, 1978.

Donat, Alexander, ed., *The Death Camp Treblinka*. New York: Holocaust Library, 1979.

Eisenberg, Azriel, *Witness to the Holocaust*. New York: The Pilgrim Press, 1981.

Fleming, Gerald, *Hitler and the Final Solution*. Berkeley: University of California Press, 1984.

Gilbert, Martin:
Auschwitz and the Allies. New York: Holt, Rinehart and Winston, 1981.
The Holocaust. New York: Holt, Rinehart and Winston, 1985.

Gutman, Israel, *The Jews of Warsaw, 1939-1943*. Transl. by Ina Friedman. Bloomington: Indiana University Press, 1982.

Gutman, Israel, ed., *Encyclopedia of the Holocaust* (Vol. 1). New York: Macmillan, 1990.

Hausner, Gideon, *Justice in Jerusalem*. New York: Harper & Row, 1966.

Hellman, Peter, *The Auschwitz Album*. New York: Random House, 1981.

Hilberg, Raul, *The Destruction of the European Jews* (3 vols., rev. ed.). New York: Holmes & Meier, 1985.

Hoess, Rudolf, *Commandant of Auschwitz*. Transl. by Constantine FitzGibbon. Cleveland: World, 1959.

Höhne, Heinz, *The Order of the Death's Head*. Transl. by Richard Barry. New York: Coward-McCann, 1969.

Kamenetsky, Ihor, *Secret Nazi Plans for Eastern Europe*. New York: Bookman, 1961.

Kaplan, Chaim A., *Scroll of Agony*. Ed. and transl. by Abraham I. Katsh. New York: Macmillan, 1965.

Keneally, Thomas, *Schindler's List*. Harmondsworth, England: Penguin Books, 1983.

Kenrick, Donald, and Grattan Puxon, *The Destiny of Europe's Gypsies*. New York: Basic Books, 1972.

Klee, Ernst, *"Euthanasie" im NS-Staat*. Frankfurt am Main: S. Fischer Verlag, 1983.

Klee, Ernst, Willi Dressen, and Volker Riess, *"Schöne Zeiten."* Frankfurt am Main: S. Fischer Verlag, 1988.

Koehl, Robert L., *RKFDV*. Cambridge: Harvard University Press, 1957.

Kraus, Ota, and Erich Kulka, *The Death Factory*. Transl. by Stephen Jolly. Oxford: Pergamon Press, 1966.

Kuznetsov, Anatolii P., *Babi Yar*. Transl. by Jacob Guralsky. New York: Dial Press, 1967.

Lang, Jochen von, ed., *Eichmann Interrogated*. Transl. by Ralph Manheim. New York: Farrar, Straus & Giroux, 1983.

Leowy, Hanno, and Gerhard Schoenberner, eds., *"Unser Einziger Weg ist Arbeit."* Frankfurt am Main: Jüdisches Museum, 1990.

Levin, Nora, *The Holocaust*. New York: Schocken Books, 1968.

Lukas, Richard C., *The Forgotten Holocaust*. Lexington: University Press of Kentucky, 1986.

Lukas, Richard C., ed., *Out of the Inferno*. Lexington: University Press of Kentucky, 1989.

Mark, Ber, *The Scrolls of Auschwitz*. Transl. by Sharon Neemani. Tel Aviv: Am Oved, 1985.

Milton, Sybil, and Roland Klemig, eds., *Bildarchiv Preussischer Kulturbesitz, Berlin* (Vol. 1 of *Archives of the Holocaust*). New York: Garland, 1990.

Moczarski, Kazimierz, *Conversations with an Executioner*. Ed. by Mariana Fitzpatrick. Englewood Cliffs, N.J.: Prentice-Hall, 1981.

Mosse, George L., *Germans and Jews*. Detroit: Wayne State University Press, 1987.

Müller, Filip, *Eyewitness Auschwitz*. Ed. and transl. by Susanne Flatauer. New York: Stein and Day, 1979.

Müller-Hill, Benno, *Murderous Science*. Transl. by George R. Fraser. Oxford: Oxford University Press, 1988.

Poteranski, Waclaw, *The Warsaw Ghetto*. Warsaw: Interpress, 1968.

Rashke, Richard, *Escape from Sobibor*. Boston: Houghton Mifflin, 1982.

Reitlinger, Gerald, *The Final Solution*. Northvale, N.J.: Jason Aronson, 1987.

Ringelblum, Emmanuel, *Notes from the Warsaw Ghetto*. Ed. and transl. by Jacob Sloan. New York: McGraw-Hill, 1958.

Rosenfeld, Harvey, *Raoul Wallenberg*. Buffalo: Prometheus Books, 1982.

St. George, George, *The Road to Babyi-Yar*. London: Neville Spearman, 1967.

Schleunes, Karl A., *The Twisted Road to Auschwitz*. Urbana: University of Illinois Press, 1970.

Schwarberg, Günther, *Das Getto*. Göttingen: Steidl Verlag, 1989.

Sereny, Gitta, *Into that Darkness*. New York: McGraw-Hill, 1974.

Stroop, Jürgen, *The Stroop Report*. Transl. by Sybil Milton. New York: Pantheon Books, 1979.

Thalmann, Rita, and Emmanuel Feinermann, *Crystal Night*. Transl. by Gilles Cremonesi. New York: Holocaust Library, 1974.

Trunk, Isaiah, *Judenrat*. New York: Macmillan, 1972.

Waite, Robert G. L., *The Psychopathic God*. New York: Basic Books, 1977.

Wiesel, Elie, *Night*. Transl. by Stella Rodway. New York: Bantam Books, 1982.

Wighton, Charles, *Heydrich*. Philadelphia: Chilton, 1962.

Wytwycky, Bohdan, *The Other Holocaust*. Washington, D.C.: The Novak Report, 1980.

Yahil, Leni, *The Holocaust*. Transl. by Ina Friedman and Haya Galai. New York: Oxford University Press, 1990.

Zimmermann, Michael, *Verfolgt, Vertrieben, Vernichtet*. Essen: Klartext, 1989.

Other Publications

Eichmann, Adolf, "Eichmann Tells His Own Damning Story." *Life*, November 28, 1960.

"Hinaus aus dem Ghetto." Jewish Museum. Frankfurt am Main: S. Fischer Verlag, 1988.

"Jüdisches Schicksal in Köln, 1918-1945." Historical Archives of the City of Cologne, 1988.

Mais, Yitzchak, ed., "A Day in the Warsaw Ghetto." Jerusalem: Yad Vashem, 1988.

Nordheimer, Jon, "For Twins of Auschwitz, Time to Unlock Secrets." *The New York Times*, April 14, 1991.

Ramsey, Winston G., ed., "The Assassination." *After the Battle*, 1979, no. 24.

Index

camp work force, 112, 120-121; SS physicians at, 102, 156, 160, 162, 164; Ukrainian guards at, 104, 110, 112, 115, 117, 120, 124, 128, 129, 131; use of freight car transport, *cover*, 108-110, *111, 113, 140. See also names of individual camps*

Donat, Alexander: 133
Draczynska, Wanda: 67
Drobless, Matti: 124
Drogobych (Ukraine): Jews killed by local police and militia in, 74

E

Eberhardt, Friedrich: 83
Edelbaum, Ben: 107-108
Edelman, Marek: 134
Ehrhardt, Sophie: and testing of Gypsies, *43*
Eichmann, Adolf: background of, 25-26; deportation of Hungarian Jews, 170, 174; as director of Reich Central Office, 32; dismay of at use of gas vans, 103; expulsion of Jews from Austria, 28, *29;* expulsion of Jews from Czechoslovakia, 30; in Palestine, 27, *29;* and planning for Jewish emigration, 26-27, 32; and transport of Jews from western Europe to death camps, 104-105; and Wallenberg, 175; at Wannsee conference, 11, 12; wedding photograph of, *29*
Einsatzgruppen: 68-73; in Baltic States, 72; and Heydrich, 69, 70, 74-75, 81, 89; and Himmler, 70, 74-76, 102; in Lithuania, 72, 74, *75;* in Soviet Union, 68-72, *73,* 74-75; in Ukraine, 72, *76-77, 78;* and Waffen-SS, 70
Estonia: German policy toward, 82
Ethnic Germans: 33-34, 62, 64, 120
Évian, France: prewar international conference on plight of Jewish refugees, 30

F

Faust, Max: *160-161*
"Final solution": and Gypsies, 13, 40, 42, 45, 46, 47, 83, 101, 103, *118-119,* 152, 165, *168, 169;* and Himmler, 25, 45, 102, 103, 104, 117, 121, 124, 131, 154, 178-181; and Hitler, 11, 25, 32, 37-38, 39, 45, 59, 63, 68, 102; planning for, 11-12, 25, 70, 89, 102
Fischer, Ludwig: 56
Foreign Office: and Madagascar Plan, 32
Foundations of the Nineteenth Century (Chamberlain): 14
France: and Jewish refugees, 30; and Madagascar Plan, 32; special insignia for Jews, 34
Frank, Hans: with fellow members of Blood Order, *69;* and liquidation of Poles, 66-67; as Nazi governor general of Poland, 34, 37, 50; with Seyss-Inquart in Warsaw, *58*
Frank, Karl-Hermann: *89*
Frankel, Leslie: 16-18
Frankfurt: past anti-Semitism in, *13;* use of police from in deportation of German

Gypsies, 45
Franz, Kurt: *122-123,* 128; attack dog of, *123*
Freiberg, Dov: 112, 115
Freikorps: 151

G

Gabcik, Josef: 90
Geneva (Switzerland): 171
Germany: economic problems following World War I, 15, 16; past anti-Semitism in, 13; traditional regard for by Russian Jews, 72. *See also* Reich
Gerstein, Kurt: 116, 167-168
Gestapo *(Geheime Staatspolizei):* and Einsatzgruppen operations, 70; and Kristallnacht, 24; and massacre at Szarajowka, 59; and RSHA, 32-33; and SS, 25; and Warsaw ghetto uprising, 159
Ghettos: Bialystok, 124, 129; Krakow, 34; Lodz, 35, 68, 98, 99, 103, 105, 107-108; Lublin, 103, 104, *111;* in Poland, 34-35, *36-37,* 68, 106, *108-109;* Theresienstadt, 165-167, 171, 178. *See also* Warsaw ghetto
Globocnik, Odilo: 102, 105, 117-118
Goebbels, Josef: anti-Jewish policies of, 19; and Kristallnacht, 23, 25, 26
Gold, Artur: 123-124
Göring, Hermann: and Aryanization program, 22; and deportation of Jews to the Government General of Poland, 34; and Jewish emigration, 28; planning for final solution, 11, 25, 102; reaction to Kristallnacht, 25
Government General of Poland: 12, 33-34, 46, 63, 66, 99, 102, 104, 107, 124, 131; proposed annexation of, 82
Great Britain: control of sea lanes by, 32; limits on Jewish immigration to Palestine, 27-28, 30; and plight of Jewish refugees, 30; trade sanction threats by, 18
Grodno (Soviet Union): Jewish transports from, *73*
Grynszpan, Herschel: 23
Gypsies: at Auschwitz, 165, *168, 169;* at Belzec, *118-119;* children at play in prewar Germany, *4-5;* estimated population in Germany, 21; and extermination, 13, 40, 42, 45, 46, 47, 83, 101, 103, *118-119,* 152, 165, *168, 169;* fate of in Ukraine, 83; initial deportations to Government General of Poland, 33-34, *44-47;* and Mengele's medical experiments, 165, *169;* Nazi policy of extermination, 5, 40, 165; and Nuremberg Laws, 21-22; origins of, 40; past persecution of, 70; registration and testing of by Reich Office for Research on Race Hygiene and Population Biology, *40-43;* resistance to SS in death camps, 47; restrictive laws in Germany, 5, 21-22, 42

H

Hackenholt, Lorenz: 115
Hadamar: euthanasia facility at, *38-39*

Haganah: prewar contacts with Eichmann, 27
Hassenberg, Arie: 172
Herder, Johann Gottfried von: 15
Heydrich, Reinhard: assassination of, 89, *90-91,* 99; and Einsatzgruppen operations, 69, 70, 74-75, 81, 89; evacuation and concentration of Jews in Government General of Poland, 32-33; funeral of, *92-93;* and Germanization of Czechoslovakia, 89; as head of SD, 26, 62; planning for final solution, 11-12, 25, 70, 89, 102; and policy for resettlement of German Jews, 28; as Reich protector for Bohemia and Moravia, *89, 90*
Himmler, Heinrich: creates network of agencies devoted to matters of race, ethnicity, and emigration, 62; designates Auschwitz as center for extermination of Jews, 151; and doctrine of Lebensraum, 62, 86; efforts to obliterate all traces of final solution, 131, 181; and Einsatzgruppen operations, 70, 74-76, 102; and final solution, 25, 45, 102, 103, 104, 117, 121, 124, 131, 154, 178-180; as head of SS, 11, 69; at Heydrich's funeral, *92-93;* on inspection tour of Auschwitz, *160-161;* and insurrections at Sobibor and Treblinka, 131; on Jews, 152; and Madagascar Plan, 32; and medical research at Auschwitz, 162, 164; orders against pilferage at camps, 120; orders to end killing operations, 178-180; policy disputes with Frank, 34; and policy of massive resettlement of Jews, 27, 64; reaction to Kristallnacht, 24-25; rivalry with Heydrich, 89, 93; and showcase camp at Theresienstadt, 167; on Slavs, 78, 86; on tour of eastern front, *78-79;* and visit to Auschwitz, 154; and visit to Treblinka, 118; and Warsaw ghetto uprising, 133
Hitler, Adolf: awards German Order posthumously to Heydrich, *93;* and definition of Jewishness, 20, 21; and deportation of Hungarian Jews, 170; and doctrine of German racial superiority, 13, 16, 38; and doctrine of Lebensraum, 16, 60, 62; euthanasia and sterilization programs, 38-39, 102; and extermination of Jews, 60, 68; and Globocnik, 117-118; instructions for invasion and administration of Poland, 63, 66; on Jewish refugees, 30; and Kristallnacht, 23-24; *Mein Kampf,* 16; and 1936 Olympic Games, 22; and Nuremberg Laws, 19, 21; orders for final solution, 11, 25, 32, 37-38, 39, 45, 59, 63, 68, 102; policy on reprisals, 85; prewar persecution of German Jews, 16-19; on Slavs, 60; suspends plans for Jewish emigration to Palestine, 28; and Ukraine, 83; use of Jews as political scapegoat, 15-16; and Warsaw ghetto uprising, 133

Military Administrative Zone on eastern front: 82

Minsk (Belorussia): executions of partisans in, *84-85;* German Jews deported to, 6; Himmler observes executions at, 75-76; Jewish transports from, 129

Mischlinge (Germans of mixed race): 12, 21

Misocz (Ukraine): mass executions of Jews in, *76-77*

Moll, Otto: 155, 168-170, 176

Monowitz (Poland): I. G. Farben facilities at, 161, 168, 172, 173. *See also* Auschwitz

Mordowicz, Czeslaw: 171

Moscow (Soviet Union): as army objective, 78

Mukachevo (Ukraine): prewar Jewish life in, *8-9*

Müller, Filip: 155, 156, 159, 169, 175, 178

Müller, Heinrich: 12

Münch, Wilhelm Hans: 162

Munich: burned synagogues in, *10*

Mussolini, Benito: 173

Mussulmans: 162

N

National Coordinating Agency for Therapeutic and Medical Establishments, 39

National Socialist German Workers' party: *See* Nazi party

Nazi party: anti-Semitism in, 60, 152; boycott of Jewish firms in Germany, 22; and concept of Lebensraum, 60-63; definition of Jews, 12, 20, 21; Ethnic Germans, resettlement of, 62, 64; and German nationalist mystique of the *Volk,* 14-15; and Kristallnacht, 23, 25; planning for final solution, 11-12, 25; policy of forced Jewish emigration, 32; racist ideology of, 13, 16, 21, 40, 60, 82-83

Netherlands: special insignia for Jews in, *34*

Night of Broken Glass: *See* Kristallnacht

Nuremberg: SA intimidation of Jews in, *19*

Nuremberg Laws: 19-22, 33

O

Oberlennigen: 25

Ohlendorf, Otto: 70, 74

Olkusz (Poland): Jewish transports to death camps, *106*

Olympic Games (1936): 22

Operation Barbarossa: 70-88; and change in German policy toward Jews, 68

Operation Reinhard: 99, 102, 103, 104; termination of, 131

Order Police: 70

Orska, Anna: 67

Otter, Baron von: 167-168

P

Palestine: Nazi plans for Jewish emigration to, 27-28, 30

Papacy: *See* Vatican

Pechersky, Alexander: 129-131

Perlasca, Giorgio: 173-174

Petranker, Giza: 128

Pfoch, Hubert: 110; photos of death-camp transport, *113*

Pinsk (Soviet Union): liquidation of Jews in, 74

Poland: anti-Semitism in, 23, 30, 102, 124-128; attitude of Nazis toward Poles, 60, 66; attitude of Poles toward Jewish fugitives in, 124-128; civilians at burial procession for Auschwitz dead, *182-183;* creation of new Jewish ghettos in by Nazis, 34, 68; deportation of Jews to death camps, *106, 107,* 108-110; establishment of camps in, 68, 99; extermination of intelligentsia in, 62, 65-66, 87; forced Jewish emigration from, 30, 32; German administration of, 12, 63-66; German reprisal policy in, 60; initial transportation and concentration of Jews and Gypsies to Government General of Poland, 32-33, 37, *44-47;* invasion and dismemberment of, 32, 33; Nazi policy of annihilation and eviction in, 63-64, *65,* 66-68; political prisoners in, 151; profiteering in, 120; railroad system in overloaded by traffic to camps, 109; resettlement of Ethnic Germans in, *64-65;* resistance activities in, 168; special insignia for Jews in, *34, 51*

Poniatowa concentration camp: *map* 33

Portugal: assistance to Hungarian Jews, 172-173

Prague (Czechoslovakia): 30; Bulovka Hospital, 93; executions in, 67; Hradcany Castle, *89, 92-93;* Saint Cyril and Saint Methodius Church, *95*

Prelle, Kurt: 22

Pronicheva, Dina Mironovna: 81

R

Race and Settlement Office (RUSHA): 12, 64

Rajzman, Samuel: 112

Rath, Ernst vom: 23, 25

Ratzel, Friedrich: 16

Reder, Rudolf: 116

Reich: administration of occupied eastern territories, 82; annexation of German-occupied Poland, 33; Christian clerical opposition to euthanasia program, 39; concentration and death camps, growing complex of, 22, *map* 33; economic recovery from Great Depression, 22; emigration of Jews from, 30-32; euthanasia program in, 38-39, 102, 103, 104, 112, 122, 123, 151; and forced labor, 11, *35,* 66, *67, 70-71,* 86; German central bank and property of concentration-camp inmates, 120; growing isolation of Jews in, 19-22, *26, 27, 34;* and Lebensraum, 13; news from troops concerning slaughter of Jews, 81-82; prewar expulsion of Polish Jews, 23, *24-25; Sippenforscher* (genealogical researchers) in, 21; sterilization program in, 38, 42

Reich Central Office of Jewish Emigration: 28, 30, 32

Reich Central Security Office (RSHA): 32, 70, 76, 89

Reich Chambers of Culture: 19

Reich Commission for the Strengthening of Germanism (RKFDV): 64

Reich Committee for Scientific Research of Hereditary and Severe Constitutional Diseases: 38

Reich Ministry for Eastern Occupied Territories: 82

Reich Office for Research on Race Hygiene and Population Biology: examination and testing by, *20, 40-43*

Rentenmark: 15

Ribbentrop, Joachim von: negotiations with France for Jewish emigration from Germany, 30

Richter, Joseph: sketches of Sobibor inmates by, *125-127*

Ringelblum, Emanuel: 35, 37, 106

Ritter, Robert: 40, *42*

RKFDV: *See* Reich Commission for the Strengthening of Germanism

Roosevelt, Franklin D.: and international conference to aid Jewish refugees, 30

Rosenberg, Alfred: 82

Rosin, Arnost: 171

RSHA: *See* Reich Central Security Office

Rumania: as Nazi wartime ally, 62; anti-Semitism in, 30

Rumkowski, Chaim: 35

Ruppin, Arthur: 22

RUSHA: *See* Race and Settlement Office

S

SA (Sturmabteilung): composition of, 11; as instrument of terror in early days of Nazi power, 18; and Kristallnacht, 11, 23-24; and nationwide boycott of Jewish businesses, *17,* 18

Sachsenhausen concentration camp: *map* 33, 151

Sandberg, Moshe: 171

Schillinger, Josef: 159

Schluch, Karl: 116

Schubert, Heinz: 74

Schumann, Horst: 162

SD (Sicherheitsdienst): 25, 26, 30, *106;* and RSHA, 32-33; and Section II 112 (subordinate bureau for Jewish affairs), 27

Secret State Police: *See* Gestapo

Security Police: 91, 96

Security Service: *See* SD

Seyss-Inquart, Artur: *58*

Shanghai (China): Jewish refugees in, 28

Siedlce (Poland): death-camp transport train at, 110, *113*

Siemens: manufacturing facilities at Auschwitz, 161

Slavs: 12, 13, 16, 151-152; Nazi attitudes toward and plans for, 60-63, 82-83, 86